MW01007856

A TOWN BUILT BY
Ski Bums

The Story of
Carrabassett Valley, Maine

**VIRGINIA M. WRIGHT AND
TOWN OF CARRABASSETT VALLEY**
Foreword by Senator Angus King

Down East Books
Camden, Maine

Down East Books

An imprint of The Globe Pequot Publishing Group, Inc.
64 South Main Street
Essex, CT 06426
www.globepequot.com

Distributed by NATIONAL BOOK NETWORK

British Library Cataloguing in Publication Information available

Library of Congress Cataloging-in-Publication Data

Names: Wright, Virginia (Virginia M.), author. | Carrabassett Valley (Me.
: Town), issuing body.
Title: A town built by ski bums : the story of Carrabassett Valley, Maine /
Virginia M. Wright, Town of Carrabassett Valley.
Description: Camden, Maine : Down East Books, 2024. | Includes
bibliographical references and index. | Summary: "Veteran journalist
Virginia Wright delves into the surprising history of a town most
passersby think is just Sugarloaf. She looks at the early days of when
Carrabassett Valley was created and at how the town's unique approach
helped it weather both boom times and downturns"— Provided by
publisher.
Identifiers: LCCN 2024021862 (print) | LCCN 2024021863 (ebook) | ISBN
9781684751792 (cloth) | ISBN 9781684751808 (epub)
Subjects: LCSH: Carrabassett Valley (Me. : Town)—History. | Carrabassett
Valley (Me. : Town)—Social life and customs. | Ski
resorts—Maine—Franklin Coungy—History. | Sugarloaf Mountain (Franklin
County, Me.)—History. | Carrabassett Valley (Me. : Town)—Biography.
Classification: LCC F29.C256 W754 2024 (print) | LCC F29.C256 (ebook) |
DDC 974.1/72—dc23/eng/20240715
LC record available at https://lccn.loc.gov/2024021862
LC ebook record available at https://lccn.loc.gov/2024021863

For Jean Luce,
whose drive, boundless energy, and unwavering trust in Carrabassett Valley's
potential are the foundation of our most audacious dreams come true.

CONTENTS

FOREWORD

Senator Angus King

BRIGADOON IS A MYTHICAL VILLAGE IN THE HIGHLANDS OF SCOTLAND that comes to life on only one day every hundred years, but on that day, as you can imagine, there is joy, celebration, and great skiing. Well, maybe not so much skiing, but that's certainly a big part of the weekly celebration at Maine's Brigadoon, Carrabassett Valley.

Every winter Friday night, the valley magically transforms into a kind of hybrid Maine town with weekend citizens from across the state, as well as from neighboring states and provinces. The population swells, parking lots fill up, and neighbors greet each other as old friends, even though they may spend most days far apart. As is true of Maine generally, there is a distinct sense of community and pride of place, especially when they look down on their friends at Sunday River from the top of Timberline.

But there is another Carrabassett as well—the year-round village with the good people who make everything work on those special weekends. Barely fifty years old, the town is home to builders and plumbers, snowmakers and chefs, fishing guides, students at Carrabassett Valley Academy, and a goodly number of retirees who have made the highlands their permanent home.

This book is the story of a magical village, from its founding as an outpost in the woods not so long ago to the present day, and why the motto on the sign outside of town still rings true: "From here on your life will never be the same."

AUTHORS AND CONTRIBUTORS

THE INITIATOR

Dick Crommett was Carrabassett Valley's unofficial town historian. He moved to his longtime seasonal home in Campbell Field in 1995 after retiring from a forty-year career in the paper industry. Active in local affairs, he was a founding member of the Carrabassett Valley Outdoor Association, a longtime member of Sugarloaf Ski Club, and a member of the Carrabassett Valley Planning Board. Friends called him the "Mayor of Campbell Field" for coordinating snowplowing and other neighborhood chores.

Dick became interested in the town's history while researching his family's genealogy. He spent several years digging into the historical record, compiling a collection of hundreds of newspaper articles, deeds, and other documents. Shortly before his death in 2004, he wrote a timeline of significant events, with the entreaty, "As the author is not immortal, he hopes that others will assume the continuing task of collecting, presenting, and preserving town historical information."

And so, in 2017, the Carrabassett Valley History Committee formed. Its original members included John McCatherin, Al Diamon, Don Fowler, Dave Cota, and Steve Pierce. Selectman John Beaupre was chairperson. Paul Crommett donated his father's research, which forms the foundation of the town's historic archives. The committee then expanded on Crommett's timeline and published it at history.carrabassettvalley.org.

The website generated so much community discussion that the committee pressed ahead with its research and hired a writer, Virginia M. Wright, who did further research and gathered the town's stories into book form.

THE WRITER

Virginia M. Wright has written about Maine's people, places, and culture for magazines and newspapers for more than thirty years. She is a former senior editor of *Down East* magazine. She lives in Camden.

THE CARRABASSETT VALLEY HISTORY COMMITTEE

John Beaupre owned and operated grocery and convenience stores in Carrabassett Valley and Kingfield for more than thirty years, including Mountainside Grocers, Ayotte's Country Store, and Sugarloaf Groceries (all of which he sold in 2022), as well as Anni's Market. He is a longtime member of the Carrabassett Valley Select Board and serves on the Golf Course Greens Committee, the Carrabassett Valley Regional Housing Committee, and the board of directors for the Carrabassett Valley Public Library. He met his wife, Tracy Allen Beaupre, at Sugarloaf Brewing Company in 2002. Their daughter, Nicole Marie Beaupre, was born in Carrabassett Valley on January 13, 1998, during the infamous 1998 ice storm.

Timothy Flight grew up as "a free-range child at Sugarloaf," and skiing and snowboarding became his passions. He was a snowboard racer at Carrabassett Valley Academy, and when he was in college, he qualified for the U.S. Alpine Nationals, winning the giant slalom event and placing first in alpine combined and second in slalom. Today, he is a computer/software systems specialist, but he is still involved in snowboard racing as CVA's snowboard supervisor. His research into his family's genealogy has taken him throughout the United States, Quebec, the Maritimes, Italy, and Ireland.

Don Fowler has skied nearly every ski area in Maine, but Sugarloaf, which he first skied as a teenager in 1957, is his North Star. He traveled to the mountain on weekends from Portland for more than three decades before moving to Carrabassett Valley and opening his Kingfield law office in the 1990s. Since then, he's skied every day the mountain is open and meticulously logged the weather, conditions, and his companions on the slopes. His knowledge of Sugarloaf history was so valuable to John Christie when he was writing *The Story of Sugarloaf* that Christie dedicated the book to him. Sugarloaf resort has frequently relied on Don's expertise in real-estate law in the western Maine mountains and, in particular, ski-area land transactions. Don is a founding member of the Carrabassett Valley Outdoor Association, a founder and former director of the Maine Ski and Snowboard Museum, and a former director and president of Mt. Abram Regional Health Center. In 2019, he was inducted into the Maine Ski Hall of Fame for his dedication to skiing and to Sugarloaf.

Ted Jones, a Millinocket native, has been a resident of Carrabassett Valley since 1966, when he became administrator assistant to Sugarloaf general manager John Christie and accountant for Sugarloaf Mountain Corporation. In 1975, he left Sugarloaf to start a wood-products manufacturing business in Kingfield. He sold the business in 1990 but continued wood-working at the home he shared with his wife, the late artist Kitty Cole Jones. Their house, built in 1956 by Dead River Company land manager Ken Packard, is a local landmark because of its bridge driveway over the Carrabassett River.

Jean Luce, her husband Norton, and their preschool children, Robert and Johanna, moved from Farmington to Sugarloaf Village in Crockertown in 1964. As a stay-at-home mom, she was the secretary of Sugarloaf Ski Club, part-time ski instructor, a founding director and later president of Sugarloaf Regional Ski Educational Foundation, and a founder and board member of Carrabassett Valley Academy. A certified ski race official, she served as race administrator of the World Cup at Sugarloaf in 1971, later officiating at twenty other World Cups, World Championships, and Olympics in the United States. In the 1980s and 1990s, Jean was on the Sugarloaf Ski Club staff as a full-time competition administrator. After retiring, Jean was a founder and president of the Maine Ski and Snowboard Museum. In 2004, she became the first woman to be inducted into the Maine Ski and Snowboard Hall of Fame.

Wendy Russell has been Carrabassett Valley's town clerk since 2006, when she, husband Scott Russell, and son Nicholas settled in the valley, which she fondly calls the "land of misfit toys" for its assortment of characters. She has lived in western Maine since 1991 and, prior to becoming town clerk, worked in area restaurants and for Sugarloaf's reservation department.

John Slagle retired full time to Carrabassett Valley in 2012 after a career that included serving as a teacher, coach, and administrator at Maine Central Institute in Pittsfield, vice president of human and environmental resources at Dragon Products in Portland, and, finally, manager in hydroelectric consulting at Kleinschmidt Associates in Falmouth. His wife, Pink, had "insisted" that their son and daughter would grow up in a skiing family. While living in Pittsfield, they made day trips to Sugarloaf; then, after moving to Scarborough in 1993, they rented seasonally on West Mountain. They bought their own place in 2001. John serves on the Carrabassett Valley Planning Board.

1

A Town Like No Other

On a few occasions, visiting feature writers, confounded in their search for a downtown with white church, historic homes, and brick storefronts, have concluded that Carrabassett Valley isn't a real town and it's just another name for Sugarloaf resort. They're wrong.

An American flag has been flown over the Carrabassett River for decades. The identity of who started the tradition is a mystery.
SAMUEL TRAFTON/MAINE DRONE IMAGING

It's true that Carrabassett Valley, located sixty country miles from Interstate 95, doesn't look like a classic rural New England town. Only a handful of buildings predate 1950. Settlement is concentrated in two areas separated by six woodsy miles: "the valley," with its 1960s A-frames and camps, and "the mountain," where Sugarloaf has built a maze of contemporary condominium and house developments, along with hotels, restaurants, and boutiques. But with just 673 year-round residents, the town of Carrabassett Valley—not Sugarloaf—owns a Robert Trent Jones Jr.–designed golf course, a two-thousand-acre ski-touring and mountain-bike park, an airport, a riverside rail trail, an advanced fitness center with indoor climbing wall and skate park, a handsome modern library, and a park with outdoor swimming pool, tennis courts, and playground.[1] Yet the town's mill rate has never exceeded $8.40.

A trail network, currently comprising eighty miles, continues to be developed by the Carrabassett Valley Trails partnership. COURTESY OF JAMIE WALTER

---

1. Population, housing, and other demographic data in this chapter were gathered from the U.S. Census Bureau's 2020 Decennial Census and 2020 American Community Survey.

That's because Carrabassett Valley doesn't just look different from other towns; it does things differently. The two dozen ski bums who founded the town in 1972 laid out a vision for an outdoor recreation economy achieved through creative investment, and townspeople have focused unwaveringly on pursuing that goal ever since. Their vision has steered them through boom times and recessions, through snow bounties and snow droughts, through the COVID-19 pandemic's travel and social-gathering restrictions, and through four ownership changes at Sugarloaf, the town's visual, cultural, and economic beating heart—but not its master. Townspeople demonstrated that point in 1993 when, with level-headedness and financial acumen, they crafted a plan to help the cash-strapped resort pay off millions of dollars in debt, all the while preserving their rock-bottom tax rate.

Today Carrabassett Valley is known far and wide not just for skiing and snowboarding but also for golfing, mountain biking, hiking,

Carrabassett Valley's motto originated with a 1968 ad for Dead River's Redington North housing development. AUTHOR

Taking a breather. COURTESY OF SAM PUNDERSON

cross-country skiing, snowshoeing, snowmobiling, ATVing, hunting, and fishing. The town's allure is such that many of the thousands who visit each year return again and again, maybe buy a seasonal home, or maybe even settle in year-round. They're responding to not only the limitless recreation but also the magnificent mountainous landscape and the camaraderie they find in a community made up almost entirely of people who share their interests.

Nearly everyone who lives in Carrabassett Valley has come from someplace else, and they're a well-educated and well-heeled lot. More than 70 percent of residents have a bachelor's degree or higher, more than twice that of the state population. The median household income of $67,000 is 30 percent higher than Franklin County households as a whole. It's a mature community, even for Maine, the oldest state: Carrabassett Valley's median age is sixty-four, whereas Maine's is forty-five (when Carrabassett was founded, the median age was late twenties to early thirties). Not surprisingly, then, Carrabassett Valley has no public school—there have

Route 27 camp. AUTHOR

never been enough children to necessitate building one, though the question has been raised now and then. Instead, the town pays the state tuition rate for children to attend the school of their choice. In 2022–2023, nearly half of the eighty-one schoolchildren living in town chose Carrabassett Valley Academy, the private ski and snowboarding school that has been an inducement for many families to relocate to Carrabassett.

The seasonal population fluctuates wildly. On peak winter weekends, an estimated ten thousand people are in town, and yet only 340 of the town's 2,100 dwelling units are occupied year-round. Most residences

5

Brackett Basin is part of Sugarloaf's side-country terrain, which is wild and remote, yet maintained and patrolled. COURTESY OF JAMIE WALTER

were built after 1985, but because all the housing developments are private, the town of Carrabassett Valley maintains and plows the same amount of roadway it did when it was founded—two and a half miles.

The built environment occupies a relatively small portion of Carrabassett Valley's fifty-one thousand acres. Six entities own nearly 85 percent of the town's land area; most of it is classified as productive forestland and is open to recreation in varying degrees, according to town manager Dave Cota. The Penobscot Nation is the largest landowner, with twenty-four thousand acres acquired from Dead River Company in 1981 with funds it received from the Maine Indian Claims Settlement Act. The Nation has long permitted recreation on its lands but closed them to the public in 2020 after town leaders testified against a bill that would grant Maine tribes full sovereignty. The select board's concern is that the proposed law exempts the Penobscots' property from local zoning and land-use ordinances. A sovereignty bill was vetoed by Governor Janet Mills in 2023, though lawmakers were expected to consider another such measure in 2024. Negotiations between the town and the Penobscot Nation are ongoing.

The Carrabassett Valley Academy campus at the foot of Sugarloaf Mountain. COURTESY OF CARRABASSETT VALLEY ACADEMY

Trails for all skill levels wind through the forest. COURTESY OF JAMIE WALTER

The state of Maine is the second largest landowner, with 9,760 acres, most of it acquired from Plum Creek Timber Company in 2013 and incorporated into the 12,045-acre Crocker Mountain Conservation Project. The town and its partners are currently expanding the Nordic skiing/mountain biking trail network into this public land. The other major landowners are Sugarloaf Mountain Corporation with 5,208 acres, the town of Carrabassett Valley with 2,261 acres, Weyerhaeuser timberland company with 2,108 acres, and the Carrabassett Valley Sanitary District with 1,347 acres.

As a relatively new town created out of unincorporated Jerusalem and Crockertown townships, which had no recorded story of longstanding settlement, Carrabassett Valley has had the advantage of starting with a clean slate. Other than timber harvesting, skiing was the town's only industry in 1972. There were no mills to revive or repurpose, no locals to alienate, no power structure to buck. Town leaders set policies and accomplished projects in unconventional ways because they were well educated, skilled in diverse occupations, and young and unfamiliar with notions of How Things Should Be Done. They forged—and their successors continue to forge—innovative cooperative relationships to achieve initiatives, such as the golf course, the trails network, and the fitness center—and that's what really sets Carrabassett Valley apart. "It's unique," said Cota, who came to Carrabassett from Greenville in 2001. "It's an amazing model."

Carrabassett Valley's partners have included the state, businesses, private institutions, and nonprofit organizations. The logistics of each collaboration were crafted to leverage each partner's resources and expertise. Recreation projects have most often been the focus, but not always. Carrabassett Valley and Sugarloaf, for example, have created what may be the country's only public/private police force: The town-employed chief oversees a staff of Sugarloaf security officers who train at the Maine Police Academy at the town's cost and who have full authority to enforce the law, including powers of arrest. "It works very well for everyone," Cota said. "The town gets a 24/7 police department for much less cost than other towns."

Of course, none of this would have happened if it were not for Carrabassett Valley's striking geology, and so we begin our history with its creation thousands of years ago.

Hole 11, part of the "string of pearls" at Sugarloaf Golf Club.
COURTESY OF SUGARLOAF

2

A Long, Long Time Ago in a Place Right Here

IN 1999, A STATE ARCHAEOLOGICAL TEAM ARMED WITH SHOVELS, BUCK-ets, and sifting screens gathered at the Hammond Field picnic area on the bank of the Carrabassett River. They had come to survey the site for evidence of past human activity and, if relics were found, advise the Maine Department of Transportation on the location of a new outhouse.

The artifacts undercovered in the Hammond Field archaelogical dig appear to be whittling and scraping tools. COURTESY OF THE MAINE HISTORIC PRESERVATION COMMISSION

A Paleo-Indian hunting party camped at the site of the present-day Route 27 rest area, leaving behind stone tools whose remnants were uncovered by archaeologists in 1999. AUTHOR

Such "shovel tests" are standard procedure in advance of government-funded construction projects, even small, unexciting ones like privies, but what the archaeologists found after they peeled back and sifted the soil wasn't mundane at all: small sandy-brown stones marked by sharp-edged multifaceted surfaces that could only have been shaped by precise strikes and pressure. They're the first recorded evidence of an ancient human presence ever found in the Carrabassett River Valley, tangible links to a nomadic band of Paleo-Indians who hunted and foraged along the river thousands of years ago.

The hunters didn't find those rocks anywhere near the Carrabassett River, though. The tools are fashioned from Onondaga chert, a hard, fine-grained sedimentary rock endemic to New York's Hudson and Mohawk river valleys, northern Pennsylvania, and southwestern Ontario. Early humans around the world favored chert because they could break it in controllable ways to make crude but durable implements for chopping, grinding, gouging, hammering, and spearing. The Hammond Field artifacts "look like whittling or scraping tools, probably used to make or sharpen other tools of bone or wood," said Arthur Speiss, chief historic preservationist at the Maine Historic Preservation Commission (MHPC), which conducted the dig. The team also uncovered "flakes" of Mount Jasper rhyolite from northern New Hampshire (flakes are stone chips removed in the toolmaking process) and a piece of calcite bone burned blue-white from having been tossed in a campfire. About four inches long, the bone was sharpened to a point and probably served as an awl. The team couldn't pinpoint the objects' age but said they may have been made as far back as the last ice age.

So how did Paleo-Indians living in western Maine twelve thousand years ago acquire chert from an outcrop hundreds of miles away? Did they carry the tools with them as they pursued caribou into new habitat opened up by shrinking glaciers? Did they acquire them in trade? Is it possible they journeyed all the way from Maine to the source of that valued rock, much the way Native peoples made long pilgrimages for Mount Kineo rhyolite, which was likewise prized for toolmaking? "I don't know," Speiss said, "and I wish we did."

Sugarloaf Mountain after a storm. SAMUEL TRAFTON/MAINE DRONE IMAGING

Nearly a decade after the Hammond Field dig, in 2008, a similar small excavation at the south end of Sugarloaf Regional Airport uncovered the remains of a likely hunting camp: one chipped tool fashioned from local stone, some fire-burned rock, and the burned bone fragments of a large mammal, perhaps a deer. Again, researchers couldn't attribute a date to the site, but it was several thousand years old and possibly used seasonally or intermittently for centuries, said Dr. Ellen Cowie, the former co-director of the Northeast Archeology Research Center, which conducted the dig for MHPC. The Carrabassett River was far from the easiest route inland, so Cowie suspects people returned to the spot because either food was abundant or it held some other significance.

As environmental-impact review projects, the Hammond Field and airport digs were not designed to answer big questions about the people who occupied the campsites, such as how they obtained food, water, and shelter, where and how far they traveled, and what their cultural and spiritual practices might have been. "There have been no such broader archaeological survey projects in Carrabassett Valley, so we do not know how many other sites there may be, nor where later [Wabanaki] settlements might have been located," Speiss said. But, he added, it wouldn't surprise him if there were more.

FIRE AND ICE

When the first people arrived in western Maine around the end of the late ice age, they encountered a landscape that had been shaped over billions of years by the pushing together and breaking apart of continents, most notably the collision 360–470 million years ago of two huge landmasses that would eventually become North America and Europe. As one tectonic plate slid under the other, the earth's crust and mantle buckled and fractured, thrusting clay and sand from the ocean depths up onto the land in huge volcanic piles that today are the Appalachian Mountains, a system of ranges stretching from central Alabama to Newfoundland and Labrador. The heat from the fiery magma that flowed over the newly formed mountains forged the ocean mud into layers of metamorphic rock, mostly granite and gabbro. In and around Carrabassett Valley, these mountains include Sugarloaf, Bigelow, Crocker, Redington, and others in the Longfellow Range, which Maine state geologist Robert Marvinney estimates were originally twelve to fifteen thousand feet high—three to four times their current elevations.

During the ice ages that followed, Maine was covered in slowly moving continental glaciers, some nearly a mile deep, similar to the ice sheets that sit atop Antarctica and Greenland today. Localized alpine glaciers whittled the high hardened stone peaks of Sugarloaf and its neighbors and crept down their slopes, carving the drainage ditch that would become the Carrabassett River. About twenty-one thousand years ago, as the climate warmed, the last of the glaciers began to recede, a process that would take over eight thousand years.

With the weight of the glaciers gone, the land rose up. Estimates vary, but the Paleo-Indians—whom Wabanaki tribes claim as their ancestors—probably arrived in western Maine during this period, about thirteen thousand years ago. "People may have been waiting for the ice to melt away," Marvinney said. "They moved in pretty quickly after the ice melted."

Maine was a subarctic environment similar to today's Labrador, with spruce forests in the southernmost part of the state gradually giving way to a treeless tundra in the north, which was covered in snow much of the year. Large herds of caribou and possibly the last of the mastodons and mammoths grazed on small plants, mosses, and shrubs that grew in the stark landscape. Paleo-Indians spent their days hunting these animals. Their small campsites, like those in Carrabassett Valley, have been found across New England and the Maritimes.

As the climate continued to warm over the next nine thousand years, dense forests of spruce, fir, poplar, birch, oak, and white pine took over Maine's interior. By the end of this phase, the landscape had assumed many of the features we'd recognize today. With these abundant resources, Native peoples' technologies advanced. They were able to travel greater distances with the canoes they built—first, dugouts chiseled and gouged from tree trunks; later, birchbark vessels capable of holding a lot of people and supplies, yet lightweight enough for long portages. They added sticks and branches to their tool-making repertoire, producing lighter and more effective hunting weapons, such as spears and bows and arrows. They fashioned cooking pots from clay, firing them to make them durable. They built villages along rivers and at the inlets and outlets of lakes and moved between settlements, summering on the coast, where fish and clams were abundant, and canoeing up rivers in the fall to winter in the interior, where game was plentiful.

The Carrabassett River Valley was almost certainly hunting ground for Native peoples over these many thousands of years. The archaeological record, though slim, supports this theory, as does the written history that begins in the sixteenth century with the arrival of European explorers and missionaries. It's unlikely, however, that the valley ever hosted anything more permanent than hunting camps for the simple reason that it wasn't a convenient place for people who traveled by foot and canoe to live. The Carrabassett is a moody waterway to navigate—a torrent in the spring, placid and rocky in summer and fall. More important, it's effectively a dead-end road: The river's headwaters between Spaulding Mountain and Mount Redington connect to no other waterway.[2] "The river doesn't go anywhere," said Kenny Wing, a retired district forest ranger, Franklin County historian, and archaeologist who has worked on digs in Maine. "Why would the Indians come here?"

Of course, the Carrabassett *does* empty into the Kennebec River, which was a major highway for Native travelers, but Wing says other tributaries provided easier access to the watershed's vast hunting grounds and beyond. The South Branch of the Dead River (where Wing, a Eustis native, has collected thousands of arrowheads and other artifacts) was a well-documented Wabanaki canoe route that linked the Rangeley Lakes to both the Kennebec in the east and, via Little Spencer Stream, the Moose River in the north. The North Branch of the Dead River connected canoeists to Quebec's Chaudière River—the same route used by Benedict Arnold for his expedition to Quebec in 1775.

Likewise, the Sandy River "is much more commodious for canoeing" than the Carrabassett, writes retired history professor David Cook in *Above the Gravel Bar: The Native Canoe Routes of Maine.* The Sandy "has

---

2. Caribou Pond didn't exist until the nineteenth century, when lumber companies formed it by damming the natural streams and wetlands.

a gentle pitch over its distance, and provides a direct Kennebec/Rangeley Lakes/Androscoggin canoe connection. At Farmington Falls, the Abenaki village of Amascontee was an easy canoe trip from Norridgewock on the main Kennebec. The Carrabassett has long and thundering rapids, while the Sandy meanders through a broad and fertile valley with canoe connections to the Belgrade/Kennebec lake system."

WHO WAS CARRABASSETT?

When the first Europeans arrived in Maine in the 1500s, the Upper Kennebec River watershed was the long-established homeland of the Abenaki Nation's Kennebec (or Canabis) tribe. The nearest village to the Carrabassett River Valley was thirty-five miles southeast—the Norridgewock (or Nanrantsouak) settlement at Old Point in Madison. There, around two hundred men, women, and children lived on a meadow on the Kennebec's east bank, just across from the mouth of the Sandy River. Their shelters, made of hemlock boughs thatched with birch bark, were clustered within a stake stockade. The Norridgewocks planted extensive cornfields along the Sandy and hunted throughout the upper Kennebec region. The Carrabassett River Valley was on a winter hunting and fishing circuit formed by the Carrabassett and Sandy rivers, which begin ten miles apart in the valleys west of the Longfellow peaks and enter the Kennebec just seven miles apart.

Sébastien Rasle, a French Jesuit missionary who lived among the Norridgewocks from 1694 to 1724, wrote rich accounts of their lifeways.[3] While he didn't refer to any river other than the Kennebec (or "Kinibiki") by name, he said that winter, when the frozen rivers and streams formed wide pathways into the forests, was a vital time for acquiring food, clothing, and furs for trade. Men donned snowshoes "made of lozenge shape, sometimes more than two feet long and a foot and a half wide," Rasle wrote in a letter to his brother in 1723. "The intention of the snowshoe is one of great utility to the savages, not only

---

3. Rasle's name appears in historical accounts as Racle, Rale, Ralé, Râle, Ralle, Roll, Ralley, and Rasles. We're following the town of Madison, where the Father Rasle Monument stands on the site of the Norridgewock village.

for running over the snow, with which the earth is covered a great part of the year, but especially for engaging in the chase of beasts, above all of the elk. These animals, larger than the largest oxen of France, go only with difficulty over the snow, so it is not difficult for the savages to overtake them." The hunters would be gone for weeks at a time, camping in wigwams that they transported on sleds.

Rasle was despised by English colonists, who accused him of encouraging the Abenaki to attack their settlements and resist their attempts to colonize the Upper Kennebec Valley. In August 1724, a Massachusetts Colony militia of 208 men under the command of Captain Johnson Harmon rowed up the Kennebec in seventeen whaleboats to what is now Winslow. From there, most of the company continued on foot to Norridgewock, intent on arresting Rasle. Instead, they committed a bloody massacre, killing the priest and, by Harmon's count, twenty-six Abenaki. In a sworn statement to the colony's lieutenant governor, Harmon reported the names of the dead, using English military titles: "The chiefs that we know among the Dead were the said Jesuit, Colonel Bomarzeen, Captain Mogg, Captain Job, Captain Carabasset, Captain Wissememet, Bomarzeen's Son-in-law, and some others whose Names I cannot Remember."

This lithograph depicts the colonial militia attack on the Abenaki settlement at Norridgewock on August 23, 1724. The Carrabassett River is believed to be named for one of the men who were killed. PUBLIC DOMAIN, VIA WIKIMEDIA COMMONS (THOMAS W. STRONG, LITHOGRAPH PUBLISHER, 98 NASSAU STREET, NEW YORK)

Are the Carrabassett River and, by extension, the town of Carrabassett Valley named for an Abenaki leader? Probably, but it's more likely a nineteenth-century fictionalized version of the man Harmon named, not the real person, about whom we've found nothing else written. The earliest recorded use of "Carrabasset River" that we've found is J. Chace, Jr. & Co.'s 1860–1862 maps of Maine and Somerset County, which show the waterway so labeled as it flows south from New Portland through Embden and North Anson and into the Kennebec.[4] To the north, in Franklin County, the river was "Seven Mile Brook," and it would continue to appear that way on maps until at least 1887.

Seven Mile Brook (or Stream or River) was English colonists' name for the entire river, from its headwaters on the flank of Sugarloaf Mountain to its confluence with the Kennebec River in North Anson. The name, which first appears in the journal of a member of Benedict Arnold's company in 1755 and persists until at least 1855, referred to the distance from Old Point to the river's mouth.

Some historians believe the Abenaki called the river, or a section of it, "Carrabassett" and that white people eventually adopted the name themselves. The more widely accepted story is that the river's name commemorates the fallen warrior named by Captain Harmon. However, nearly all names of people and places recorded by the English and French are corruptions of Wabanaki words; the tribes themselves had no written forms of their languages. White people used inventive spellings and, often, incorrect meanings, which have been further corrupted over time.

So, did Harmon get the man's name right? Penobscot language scholar Frank Siebert didn't think so.[5] In a 1941 letter to Maine historian Fannie Hardy Eckstorm, Siebert commented that clan names had become confused with identifiers used by white people. "The Sturgeon gens had their hunting territory on the Kennebec according to my informants and

---

4. The spelling of Carrabassett wasn't standardized until the early twentieth century. Before that, it appears on maps and in newspaper and historical accounts variously as Carabasset, Carrabasset, and Carrabassett.

5. Frank Thomas Siebert Jr. (1912–1998) published a Penobscot dictionary with fifteen thousand entries in 1984. A pathologist, he was a self-taught linguist dedicated to preserving the Penobscot language, even moving to the neighboring Indian Island community of Old Town after his retirement in the 1970s to pursue his research.

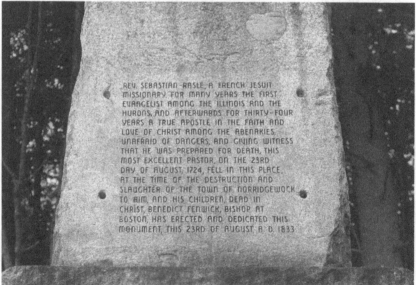

REV. SEBASTIAN RASLE, A FRENCH JESUIT
MISSIONARY FOR MANY YEARS THE FIRST
EVANGELIST AMONG THE ILLINOIS AND THE
HURONS, AND AFTERWARDS FOR THIRTY-FOUR
YEARS A TRUE APOSTLE IN THE FAITH AND
LOVE OF CHRIST AMONG THE ABENAKIES,
UNAFRAID OF DANGERS, AND GIVING WITNESS
THAT HE WAS PREPARED FOR DEATH, THIS
MOST EXCELLENT PASTOR, ON THE 23RD
DAY OF AUGUST, 1724, FELL IN THIS PLACE,
AT THE TIME OF THE DESTRUCTION AND
SLAUGHTER OF THE TOWN OF NORRIDGEWOCK
TO HIM, AND HIS CHILDREN, DEAD IN
CHRIST, BENEDICT FENWICK, BISHOP AT
BOSTON, HAS ERECTED AND DEDICATED THIS
MONUMENT, THIS 23RD OF AUGUST A.D. 1833

This granite monument at Old Point in Madison marks the site of an Abenaki village that was abandoned after an attack by a colonial militia in 1724. AUTHOR

historical evidence," Siebert offered by way of example. "Witness 'Carabasset' killed at Norridgewock—really *kabásse*, [meaning] sturgeon." In his 1962 book, *Indian Place Names of New England*, John Huden also noted the similarity between "Carrabassett" and the Abenaki word for sturgeon, which he spelled *kabassa*. Huden, who studied New England Indian history for forty years and was familiar with several Algonquin dialects, suggested—with a question mark—that "Carrabassett" translates as "sturgeon place." In 2016, Steve Pinkham, the author of *Mountains of Maine: Intriguing Stories Behind Their Names*, consulted with Carol Dana, linguistics specialist for the Penobscots, who speculated that "Carrabassett" could have been derived from a Wabanaki word meaning "one who turns around quickly," possibly because the man was particularly agile at fighting or hunting.

If the river does draw its name from a fallen warrior, it probably wasn't the Abenakis' doing. "The Euro-American way to name a place is either by naming it after someone, or naming for another place," writes Penobscot historian James Francis in the foreword to *Above the Gravel Bar*. The Penobscots and the Abenaki are both members of the Wabanaki Confederacy of Eastern Algonquian nations, which have similar languages, spiritual beliefs, and lifeways. "Penobscots had three basic ways of naming a particular location. Places were named for their geography or geology, the resources found there, or their names are based on legends that were passed down from generation to generation." Indeed, Native American tribes across the country didn't consider humans significant enough to lend their names to the land. They named locations for their defining characteristics—the landmarks or essence of place that would tell a voyager where he was.

The man Harmon called "Carrabasset" doesn't appear again in written history until the mid-nineteenth century, when Maine lawyer, poet, and dramatist Nathaniel Deering reinvented him as a survivor. From 1822 to 1836, Deering worked in a law office overlooking the Kennebec River in Skowhegan about ten miles downriver from Old Point. While there, he became interested in the Norridgewock story and wrote his first play, *Carabasset or the Last of the Norridgewocks*. Published in 1830, it's the fictional tale of Chief Carabasset, "the best and bravest of the

Norridgewocks," who survives the English attack and vows revenge for the murders of his wife and child, only to throw himself off a cliff at the end. *Carabasset* received positive reviews in Portland and Boston, as well as praise (but not a prize) from New York actor Edwin Forrest's playwriting-contest committee. *Carabasset* went on to have a decades-long afterlife in Maine classrooms. In 1912, a *Portland Sunday Telegram* columnist declared that that all the schoolboys of his generation could recite some of *Carabasset*'s lines.

Deering's *Carabasset*, along with two popular poems about the Nor-ridgewock attack by John Greenleaf Whittier, "did more than merely entertain readers and audiences, they also inspired a whole new genera-tion's interest in Norridgewock" and have sometimes been mistaken for historical fact, according to Ashley Elizabeth Smith, an assistant professor of Native American studies at Hampshire College in Amherst, Massa-chusetts, and a descendant of Norridgewock villagers. In her 2017 Colby College dissertation, Smith, a Madison native, writes, "Shortly follow-ing the publication and performances of *Carabasset* in 1831, some locals from the town of Norridgewock, including historian William Allen, col-laborated with Bishop Fenwick of the archdiocese of Boston to erect a monument in honor of Father Rasle at the site of his church and burial at Old Point. In the same year, John Pickering edited and published Rasle's manuscript, *Dictionary of the Abenaki Language*. Documents regarding and essays about Norridgewock, the Indian wars, and Rasle proliferated in the early collections of the Maine Historical Society around the same time. These early literary works and histories are also repeated at length in later works, often copied word for word. By repeating the stories, his-torians and literary authors participated in a sort of ritual that claims a national historical tradition which they are simultaneously creating."

During this Norridgewock resurgence, the name "Carrabassett" was given to three vessels between 1830 and the early 1900s (a merchant brig, a Union Navy side-wheel steamer, and a Coast Guard cutter); a marching song in the 1840s; a Masonic lodge in Canaan in 1844; an Indian chief in Nathaniel Harrington Bannister's *Ethan Allen, or the Green Mountain Boys of 1775*, which opened at New York's Bowery Theatre in February 1847; a harness-racing horse in the 1870s; and—we're not kidding—a maid in an amateur production of the British farce *Peg Woffington* in Honesdale, Pennsylvania, in 1895 (in the original script, the maid is unnamed).

The name also was given to the former Fifteen Mile Stream in Canaan, Skowhegan's neighbor. That's right: There are *two* Kennebec River tributaries that have been renamed Carrabassett. Canaan's Carrabassett Stream flows south from Sibley Pond, through Canaan village, along the Skowhegan border, and into the Kennebec County town of Clinton, where it empties into the Kennebec. In 1790, surveyor Samuel Weston drew it on his map as Fifteen Mile Stream—fifteen miles is not the brook's length, but rather the distance between its mouth and, you guessed it, Old Point. By the late 1840s, Canaanites were calling the stream by the name the playwright in the town next door had recently made famous: Carrabassett. J. Chace Jr.'s 1860 map of Maine shows that the stream had a different name—Sabbatas Creek—once it passed into Kennebec County, just as it shows the Carrabassett River had a different name—Seven Mile Brook—once it passed into Franklin County.

Chace's maps were effectively official stamps of approval. The county maps were branding and marketing tools that, according to the Osher Map Library, "promoted and affirmed a shared sense of community on a regional, local, and individual scale through a mode of interconnectedness experienced like never before. They functioned as important indicators of regional identity and cultural change." The state map, commissioned by Governor Israel Washburn Jr. and published in 1862, was an even bigger deal. Never before had Maine been mapped in such detail—nearly every road, railroad, hill, mountain, harbor, pond, river, and stream in every city and town was identified. "For accuracy, fullness and beauty of execution, it is unsurpassed, if not unequalled, by the map of any State in the Union," Washburn said in his 1862 address to the state.

In 1911, the *Correct Orthography of Geographic Names* by the United States Board on Geographic Names listed "Carrabassett Stream" as the preferred designation for the entire river, rejecting other spellings and classifications like "Carrabasset," "Carrabasset River," "Sevenmile River" and "Seven Mile Brook."

By the time the Seven Mile Brook became the Carrabassett River, there hadn't been a Wabanaki settlement in the Upper Kennebec Valley for more than one hundred years. After Harmon's massacre, the Norridgewock Abenakis relocated to Wabanaki communities elsewhere in Maine and in Quebec. Contrary to popular belief, however, they didn't vanish from the region, Smith says. Small groups, including members of Smith's family, eventually returned to their homeland, and Wabanaki people regard it as a place of spiritual and historical importance to this day.

Al Diamon, a former member of the Carrabassett Valley History Committee, contributed to this chapter.

Interlude
LIFE IN A 1930s CARRABASSETT LOGGING CAMP

Ken Packard worked as a woodsman in the Dead River region, most of it as Dead River Company's head of operations in the Carrabassett River Valley, from 1938 until his retirement around 1973. Packard describes lumber camps of the 1930s in this excerpt from a 1971 interview conducted by University of Maine folklore student (and Sugarloafer) Jill Allen. The text has been edited for length and clarity.

I lived in a logging camp a good deal in my younger days. It was a great many times laid up out of logs. They used different methods of building a camp. Sometimes they'd build a board camp. They'd just set up studding and put boards around and tarred paper on the outside for one year. If they expected to be there several years, then they laid up a log camp, and it was very comfortable when it was chinked in good shape.

They had a camp for the men to sleep in, a camp known as the cook room, and, between them, what was known as the dingle, which was covered—a roof over it. That housed the supplies that wouldn't freeze—flour, sugar, molasses, kerosine, and such things.

The floors were pole floors adzed down some to level the floor off a little, but you still didn't want to stub your toe too much or you'd fall down. In the cook room between the tables, they had boards on the floor, but under the tables, there were pole floors.

We had plenty of sugar and all kinds of meats. The cooks made all the breads—biscuits and yeast breads. The French cooks were real strong on that.

A Maine logging camp is depicted in this postcard bearing a 1906 postal stamp.
COURTESY OF JAY AND WENDY WYMAN

When the men got up for breakfast, they had to be washed up and shaven, or the cook wouldn't let them in. They had to keep their clothes reasonably clean. Once in a while we did get into a camp where they had cooties [lice]. I never got them on me but just once, and that was after I started to run a camp [in Jerusalem] for Dead River Company, and I gave up my office for another man and his wife, who were coming up to do some work for us.

People didn't bring their street clothes to camp. They just brought their work clothes—big rubbers and stockings, shirts, and heavy britches. After a stormy day, the men's camp was pretty well steamed up with their laundry drying on the stove.

Ordinarily on Sunday, there were two or three old-fashioned scrub boards and wash tubs. You could heat water in the men's camp or they had a big kettle out of doors where they'd build a fire and wash their clothes. That was their entertainment on Sunday.

In the evening, they'd find a piece of wood that'd make a good axe handle—a good piece of hard rock maple. They used knives and draw shaves [to whittle the wood], and they took pride in seeing who could make the best axe handle.

Lumberman's Life Series, Harold Tague and Kenneth Packard, interviewed by Jill Allen. Northeast Archives of Folklore and Oral History, na0705, courtesy of Fogler Library, University of Maine, umaine.edu/folklife/archives/mf-012-lumbermans-life-collection/

3

Opening the Wilderness

IN THE WINTER OF 1874, AS THE COUNTRY SANK DEEPER INTO AN ECO-
nomic depression, the forest north of Kingfield bristled with the promise of prosperity. Three hundred choppers, sawyers, and swampers were
in the snowy woods of Jerusalem Township, rough-cutting roads, felling
trees, and stacking logs high onto horse-drawn sleighs, which teamsters
then delivered to the Carrabassett's banks. The piney scent of freshly cut
wood mingled with the aroma of pork and beans and baking bread at
nine crude camps that had been constructed a few months earlier for the
Franklin Land & Lumber Company's first season of business. Organized
by Boston coal importer Howard Snelling, Franklin Land & Lumber was
not Jerusalem's first logging operation, but it was by far the largest. The
company had purchased all of Jerusalem and a portion of Crockertown,
and its arrival ushered in an intense—if brief—era of corporate lumbering and railroading that would transform the Carrabassett River Valley.

Thousands of logs drifted partway downriver during a January thaw;
then, as temperatures plummeted, they formed an ice-caked jam so tight
a person could walk across the river on it. On the riverbanks near where
the men were working, the lumber had been frost-heaved into disorderly
heaps, logs pointing in all directions. By April 1, the Franklin Company
woodsmen had stacked twelve million board feet of logs and one hundred
thousand railroad ties along the river's edge for three miles.[6] Over the

---

6. Then, as now, the lumber content in a log was determined with scaling sticks. A "board foot" is
$12 \times 12 \times 1$ inches. So how many logs are in twelve million board feet? It all depends on the length
and diameter of the logs, but here's a rough picture: There are four hundred board feet in a sixteen-
foot-long log with an average diameter of twenty-four inches. It would take thirty thousand of them
to yield twelve million board feet.

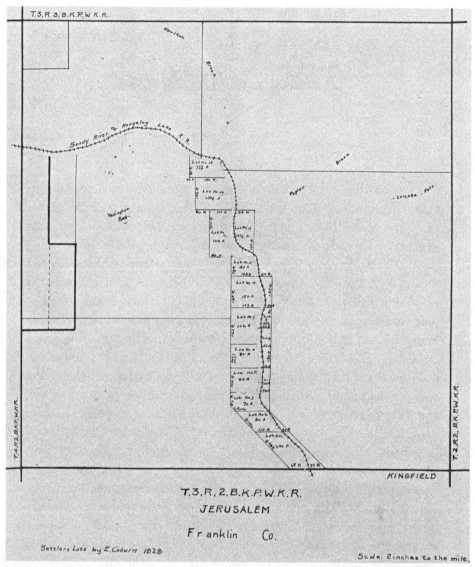

A state survey map of Jerusalem Township and the fifteen settlers lots that were laid out from the Kingfield town line to the location of present-day Huse Mill Road in 1828.

The Lawrence Plywood Mill. COURTESY OF JAY AND WENDY WYMAN

next few weeks, the stacks grew in number and height. Come the spring freshet, the woodsmen would roll the logs into the river and open the dams, and log drivers in bateaux would run the lumber down the Kennebec River, the railroad ties to Fairfield, the pine and spruce to Augusta, Hallowell, and Bath, where mills would saw them into boards for shipment to Boston, New York, and Liverpool, England.

That was the plan, anyway, but the early thaw had expensive—and deadly—consequences. When the logs were pushed into the river, there wasn't enough water to carry them downstream. They quickly snagged on the rocks, tumbling over each other and piling so high and tight that they choked the river. Water backed up behind the massive jam and spilled over the banks. Two log runners who tried to dislodge the snarl fell into the icy river and drowned when logs passed over them. Reporting on the second fatality, the May 28 *Daily Kennebec Journal* wrote, "His name was Savage, from New Brunswick. He was of the firm of Anderson & Savage, who were operators this winter in hauling lumber for the Franklin Land & Lumber Co. and had charge of a section of the drive. They were breaking a jam when its head fell down, letting Mr. Savage and another man into quick water. When they were got out, both were supposed to be dead, but the efforts to resuscitate them were successful in the case of the second man, but Mr. Savage had passed the line of life."

The concrete pad on the east bank of the Carrabassett River just below the town office is a remnant of the Lawrence Plywood mill. AUTHOR

A few days later, under pressure from the river drivers, the company called a halt to the drive and discharged the crew. Logs and railroad ties were strewn like giant pick-up sticks in the Carrabassett for miles. They'd sit there for an entire year.

A BAD TRACT OF COUNTRY

Jerusalem's official designation was "Township 3, Range 2, Bingham's Kennebec Purchase, West of the Kennebec River," an intimidating and yet plainly descriptive mouthful that revealed its lineage.[7] The township was drawn out of a one-million-acre Upper Kennebec Valley tract that wealthy Philadelphia land speculator William Bingham had purchased, along with another million acres east of the Penobscot River, from the debt-ridden state of Massachusetts for $311,250, or about 12.5 cents an acre, in 1793. As part of the bargain, Bingham was to establish 2,500

---

7. On maps, it was a breezy T3 R2 BKP WKR.

settlers on his lands within ten years, boosting Maine's population by 25 percent. He hoped to make a substantial profit selling parcels for 50 cents to $1 an acre, but the lots proved a tough sell. It's not as if he hadn't been warned. He'd seen Captain William W. Morris's summary of his 1792 survey of the Kennebec lands. "A bad tract of country," Morris had written, and he specifically mentioned the Longfellow Range. "This chain of mountains occupies a large portion of the tract on the west side of the river, and but little of the land not included in it is fit for cultivation."

With more lucrative investments to occupy him, Bingham grew uninterested in his Kennebec purchase and eventually retired to England, where he died at age fifty-one in 1804. The trustees of his estate—his five sons-in-law—worked out an arrangement with the state of Massachusetts that allowed them to sell timberlands instead of farmlands. By the middle of the nineteenth century, they had disposed of most of the Maine holdings, including, in 1828, 1,457 acres on both sides of the Carrabassett River. Jerusalem was divided into fifteen settlers' lots laid out from the Kingfield line to the present-day location of Huse Mill Road.[8] By 1837, fifty-four people from eight families were living in Jerusalem, and a sawmill was operating on the Carrabassett's bank, according to the late Carrabassett Valley historian Dick Crommett. A special state census reported no settlers in Crockertown that year, but by 1840 six residents had set down roots. For the next thirty years, neither township grew.[9] In fact, Jerusalem was down to just thirty-two souls when Franklin Land & Lumber engineers began clearing the Carrabassett of large rocks and other obstacles and building dams in late summer of 1873.[10] When the three hundred loggers arrived a few months later, the population jumped a hundredfold.

At the time, logs harvested in Maine were delivered to their owners almost exclusively by driving them downstream on the spring freshet.

---

8. Not to be confused with the Settlers' Lots housing development off Route 27, which gets only its name from the original settlers' lots.

9. Crockertown (or Crocker Township) was Township 4, Range 2, Bingham's Kennebec Purchase, West of the Kennebec River. It was named for Isaac Crocker, an early landowner. In 1967, the state legislature renamed the township Sugarloaf.

10. In October, some of Jerusalem's new dams gave out, forcing farmers downriver to boat their sheep off the flooded intervales.

Prouty-Miller mill ruins in the woods just north of the Access Road. AUTHOR

"The best sort of spring provided a slow gradual melt of the winter cover to give a steady flow of water into the streams, and then the logs would come down with little trouble," writes David C. Smith in *A History of Lumbering* in Maine. "Too early a spring would provide an early freshet, and the logs might hang for lack of water later on. Such a year was 1874, and observers were acutely aware of the possibilities. As one said, 'Good judges state that many drives of logs on small streams will hang up this spring, and those who work on small capital will be in danger of meeting with embarrassment in consequence.'"

A logging truck in the valley in 1946. COURTESY OF SUSAN HARRISON

Embarrassment was the least of the rivermen's concerns. Shepherding logs downstream was miserable and dangerous work. The men worked sixteen hours a day, seven days a week, jumping across bobbing logs to steer and separate them with hooked poles called peaveys. Often, they waded chest-deep in icy water to "card the ledges"—that is, drag heavy, slippery logs off rocks. When there was a jam, they'd pick their way across the pileup and use poles to pry loose the "key logs." If that didn't work, they blasted the tangle with dynamite. Only rarely did they walk away, as the river drivers did in Jerusalem in spring of 1874. Nothing would move those logs without high water.

Franklin Land & Lumber hoped to get another shot at running the logs in November, typically Maine's wettest month, but the drought persisted. Nevertheless, the company sent fifteen men to repair dams and camps and cut roads for a reduced winter campaign. Over the next few months, a crew of fifty woodsmen cut two million board feet of spruce and stacked the logs alongside the clogged river in anxious anticipation of the spring freshet.

As the thaw approached, Franklin Land & Lumber took no chances, calling in a new team of rivermen—hotshots from the self-proclaimed

1900

Last Monday, the Crockertown mill was shut down on account of the breaking of the cable. Monday night about 20 of the employees of the mill went to Stratton and brought home a terrible "load," some being drunk, others were carrying it with them. During the evening, things got very much stirred up. They enjoyed singing, buck and wing dancing, and in fact everything was going on full blast. The rioting became so hot that the proprietor of the boarding house, Mr. Robert Fossey, drove to Kingfield, and he together with Deputy Sheriff Bert Small settled the affray. Up to this writing, only one arrest has been made.
—*Phillips Phonograph*, September 28

Lumber Capital of the World. "As soon as the ice was out, a crew of 225 drivers, Abner West of Bethel, the 'boss' driver, went from Bangor to Carrabassett river, or Seven Mile Brook, as it is called on the map, and have driven 11 million feet of logs into the Kennebec, which had been left in the most difficult condition to handle," the *Bangor Whig and Courier* reported on May 27, 1875.[11] The newspaper then indulged in a little home-team boasting: "The crew returned yesterday feeling particularly well pleased with their achievement, having accomplished what a crew of Kennebec drivers failed to do last season after losing two men."

RAILROAD FEVER

When the Billerica & Bedford narrow-gauge railway in Massachusetts went belly up in 1878, Franklin County business leaders saw an opportunity to begin building the rail network they'd been talking about for nearly thirty years. They envisioned a symbiotic relationship between lumber and railroad interests: With new lines extending from Maine Central in Farmington, lumber companies would gain access to the Upper Kennebec Valley's vast timberlands, rich in white and yellow birch, rock maple, spruce, and poplar. In turn, the railroad would be largely supported by revenue from transporting logs and sawn lumber. Investors snapped up the failed B&B's iron rail, along with two engines, two passenger cars, and five platform cars, and in November 1879, a train chugged over the eighteen-mile Sandy River Railroad (SRR), from Farmington to Phillips, for the first time.

The project didn't cure Franklin County's railroad fever; it fanned it. Within a year, business leaders were agitating for logging lines through the Carrabassett and Dead River valleys. Among the proponents of a route connecting the SRR to Jerusalem: Samuel W. Sargent, the leader of a group of Boston businessmen who had purchased Franklin Land & Lumber in January 1878 for $60,000. The company, now called Carrabassett Land & Lumber, was manufacturing up to five million shingles

---

11. Like many lumbermen, Abner West was a farmer who earned supplementary income in the winter logging trade. Throughout the year that the logs were stranded, newspaper estimates varied from eleven million to fifteen million board feet.

a year in addition to cutting trees. Horse-drawn wagons were the only way to get the shingles out of the valley and down to the Maine Central Railroad station in Farmington, a transportation chain that required three landings in just twenty-five miles: teams hauled the shingles to King-field, where they were reloaded onto another set of wagons for transport to Strong, where they were reloaded onto the Sandy River Railroad and driven to Farmington, where they reloaded onto the Maine Central. Eager to streamline the process—and minimize his company's reliance on fickle spring freshets for moving logs—Sargent went on the hustings as president of the proposed Franklin & Megantic Railway. In March 1883, he met with the editors of the *Lewiston Evening Journal*, who pushed his case to their readers: The railroad would bring prosperity to towns along its route, the newspaper said, and investors would be easy to find given the immense amount of freight to be shipped from Sargent's "large and powerful" company and the thousands of acres of timberlands yet to be broken. "There is still another reason why a railroad to those points would pay: the Dead River region—Tim Pond is there, places than which is none better in this beautiful state. For fishing or for hunting, there are many who prefer the Dead River region to Rangeley, and especially in this case with those who go away to escape the crowd."

The campaign succeeded. Though a few other routes were hotly debated in stakeholder towns that year, the Franklin & Megantic (F&M) prevailed. A fifteen-mile line from Strong to Kingfield opened to traffic on December 10, 1884; it had two engines, one passenger car, one express/mail car, and thirty-two freight cars. As predicted, over the next few years, numerous mills popped up and hundreds of acres of timberlands were broken in the region served by the F&M. Kingfield alone boasted several new mills turning out birch dowels, shingles, clapboards, and other wood products. In Jerusalem, lumber crews cut a road to the lower Dead River, so freight could be hauled to the railroad terminus in Kingfield. This route became what is known today as Carriage Road.

The cleared land attracted the valley's first farmers. In Crockertown, Charles G. Campbell and Asa U. Baker, immigrants from New Brunswick by way of Kingfield, farmed 150 acres in the area known to today as Campbell Field. In Jerusalem, Joseph Cleaves had a farm near what is now Sugarloaf Regional Airport.[12] "Most of the farms here were small family farms that sprang up to help the log companies with their horses," Kenny Wing says. "Logging was a winter venture, and the horses needed a place to stay in the summer. The farmers would fatten them up, and they'd be ready for the fall. Cleaves might have put milk on the train, but for the most part, these were subsistence farms that sold only locally."

In the meantime, Franklin County was gaining a statewide reputation for its narrow-gauge network. "The peculiarity is not in the kind of railroads that we have, for there are several of the popular little two-foot gauge roads now running, but in the fact that commencing at Farmington and ending at Kingfield and Rangeley, are three complete railroads beginning and ending in the county: the Sandy River, from Farmington to Phillips, the Franklin & Megantic from Strong to Kingfield, and now the Phillips and Rangeley that will soon be complete to Rangeley village," the *Phillips Phonograph* observed on October 17, 1889. The newspaper then launched into a pitch for fulfilling Samuel Sargent's original vision by extending the F&M eight miles from Kingfield to Jerusalem, where Drew's Mill was manufacturing shingles on the Carrabassett's west bank. "This would greatly increase the wealth of the county above Kingfield, which would benefit the town very much. And then there are millions upon millions of birch in this township and plenty of good water powers on the Carrabassett upon which mills might be run successfully if the railroad could be reached easier."

Thus Sargent's campaign was reignited, though Sargent was no longer involved. Carrabassett Land & Lumber Company had folded, a casualty of the Howard Snelling company bankruptcy in 1886. Sargent and a partner had taken over the ailing Boston coal-import business after Snelling was killed in a train-and-carriage accident in 1879. Though it had no debts of its own, Carrabassett Land & Lumber became entangled in the messy finances. Franklin County eventually took possession of the company's Jerusalem and Crockertown lands and mill and sold them to Frank D. J. Barnjum, the "Maine lumber king," in 1893. Like Sargent

---

12. This section of Jerusalem was sometimes called "Cleaves" or "Drew's Mill," as in "A crew has cut a winter road through from Cleaves to lower Dead River." Once the railroad was built and a small village sprouted around the station, the area was known as Carrabassett.

1904

Report comes from Parker Sanborn's camps in Bigelow of a spruce recently cut by Ed Laney's crew, which was 102 feet long and 7 feet in diameter at the top. Mr. Sanborn is reported as saying that this is the largest spruce he has seen in the 15 or 20 years of his lumbering experience. The log was cut into short lengths and hauled to the mill of Prouty & Miller in Bigelow.
—*Independent–Reporter*, December 15

before him, Barnjum headed up a group of landowners advocating for an extension of the F&M.[13]

McGregor Brothers of Rumford was contracted to clear and grade a route between Kingfield and Drew's Mill. It hired 150 laborers, 65 of them Italian immigrants in the charge of Pelham, New York, *padrone*—or labor agent—Frank Musello. The Italians arrived at the Maine Central Railroad station in Farmington at noon on an early August day, where they were met by curious onlookers: "The crowd at the depot was afforded much amusement while the aliens poured out of their train and boarded another on the Sandy River," the *Franklin Journal* reported.

At the time, the bank panic of 1893 had plunged the country into another depression. Unemployment in Maine was high, and homeless men (or "tramps," as the *Journal* called them) were showing up in Farmington almost daily in search of work on the F&M. So why did McGregor Brothers import a crew of Italians from New York? Probably because they were easy to exploit. Between 1880 and 1900, one million Italians immigrated to the United States, thousands of them to Maine, seeking a better life after decades of social unrest and widespread poverty in their own country. By some accounts, the padrones, who recruited from villages in Italy, were little better than slave traders. "Critics cited the often-absolute dependency of the non-English-speaking peasant laborers, who relied on

---

13. The extension was chartered as the Kingfield & Dead River Railroad, but that was little more than a corporate identity; everyone referred to it as the F&M.

their padroni as travel agents, with fees reimbursed from pay checks; as landlords, even of shacks and box cars; as storekeepers often on exorbitant credit; and as bankers," writes historian Alfred T. Banfield in the journal *Maine History*. "In Maine, the padrone system operated to the fullest. It channeled large numbers of Italians into Maine to build railroads, construct dams and mills, and cut granite, often amid labor unrest."

Not that the Italians were pushovers. On some occasions when contractors failed or tried not to pay, they responded with strikes and riots. In Montreal, for example, seven hundred Italian railroad laborers rioted after working without pay for more than a month in 1888. That same year, five hundred Italians demanding two months' back pay went on strike against the Upper Coos railroad in New Hampshire. The disputes in Franklin County were not so large, but the F&M was not immune and the labor practices that provoked them were much the same. In 1885, an Italian rail gang, angry about the amount of grocery money being garnished from their wages, threw trees across the track in West Freeman and detained a train for four hours.

On the afternoon of November 10, 1883, the Italians were dismissed from the F&M job site. The last crew to leave attracted attention at the train depot in Kingfield just as they had when they arrived in Farmington three and half months earlier. "It made business on the breadline good for Mr. Bates, the baker," the *Farmington Chronicle* remarked. Their stint in the Carrabassett River Valley was unmarred by complaints about wages or cruel bosses, but this would not be the end of protests over working conditions while building the F&M.

Frank J. D. Barnjum, Maine's Lumber King

For a short time at the turn of the twentieth century, one man owned nearly all the 49,664 acres that make up present-day Carrabassett Valley—and that was just a fraction of Frank John Dixie Barnjum's holdings in Maine and Canada. Buying and selling timberlands made the "Maine lumber king" a fortune, and in the latter part of his life, Barnjum personified enlightened self-interest as he devoted his energies to forest conservation, warning of a "wood famine" and devastating climatic changes if the lumber industry failed to curb its "ruthless deforestation."

Born in Montreal in 1856, Barnjum purchased Jerusalem Township (about twenty-three thousand acres) from the Carrabassett Land & Lumber Company in 1893. Three years later, he purchased twenty thousand acres in Crockertown. There, near what would become Bigelow village, his Crockertown Lumber Company pioneered the use of portable sawmills in the woods. By 1913, Barnjum had control of nearly all the timberlands around the Sandy River & Rangeley Lakes and Franklin & Megantic railroads—nearly three hundred thousand acres in all. He also had extensive holdings in Nova Scotia, Cape Breton, and British Columbia.

Barnjum had homes in Lynnfield, Massachusetts, and in Kingfield, first on Salem Road and later on Blanchard Hill Road. His wife, Bertha, and their children stayed at one of these residences while Barnjum traveled for business—to Old Town, where he had a sawmill; to Annapolis, Nova Scotia, where he had another home and timberlands; to Montreal, where he had an office; to British Columbia, where he had still more timberlands and yet another home; and to Bangor, Boston, and New York.

In 1922, he made news when he offered a $5,000 prize for a practical method of combating and suppressing the spruce bud worm, which had caused tremendous damage to the forests of the United States and Canada. In Maine alone, the spruce budworm infestation killed 40 percent of the spruce and 70 percent of the fir—about 27.5 million cords of wood—between 1915 and 1922.

After his retirement at age sixty, Barnjum traveled to other countries to learn about their woodlands management practices, good and bad, and wrote articles for newspapers and other publications about what he'd observed overseas and about the need for forest conservation, which he considered vital to the lumber industry's survival. He died at age seventy-seven in Paris, just after a visit to Italy at the invitation of that country's chief of the forest service.

Interlude

CARRABASSETT VALLEY MILLS

Carrabassett Land & Lumber Company manufactured shingles on Brackett Stream, near where the Carrabassett Valley Academy dorm stands today. A group of Boston businessmen led by Samuel W. Sargent formed the company from Franklin Land & Lumber, which they purchased in 1878 and renamed, building a shingle mill sometime later. Sargent was a staunch proponent of extending narrow-gauge rail service from Strong to Kingfield and Jerusalem. Franklin County took the company timberlands, which included all of Jerusalem and part of Crockertown, for non-payment of taxes, and it sold them to lumber king Frank Barnjum in 1893.

Crockertown Lumber Company was among the first to use portable sawmills in the Maine woods. In late fall of 1899, it erected two of them near Bigelow Station to handle what the *Phillips Phonograph* called "the most extensive lumbering operations ever seen at this section." Easily dismantled and reassembled within a few days, portable mills were favored for lumbering large lots in areas where river driving was especially difficult. Once the lot was cleared, the mill was moved to the next timbering area. Each of Crockertown's mills had the capacity to saw twenty-five thousand board feet of lumber a day. Owned by a group of investors headed by Frank Barnjum, the company timed its start-up with the extension of the Franklin & Megantic Railway line from Jerusalem, which hauled away up to twenty-five carloads of Crockertown lumber every day. Bigelow Station was built opposite the mill in the summer of 1900, giving the village that grew up around it its name. Crockertown Lumber was among seventy-nine defendants (all sawmill operators) in the 1901–1902 "Sawdust Case." The lawsuit, which attracted national interest, was brought by owners of pulp and cotton mills on the Kennebec River in Winslow and Waterville, who complained that sawdust thrown into the river and its tributaries clogged their runways and wheels. Maine Supreme Court Justice William Penn Whitehouse granted a perpetual injunction against the sawmill owners, restraining them from throwing refuse into the river. Crockertown Lumber sold its mill and timberlands to Prouty & Miller in 1902.

Drew's Mill (a.k.a. Grant Mill and Emerson Mill) was built by Craig Drew of Skowhegan in 1878 on the west side of the Carrabassett River, opposite where the Carrabassett Valley Town Office stands today. There you can see large cuboid mounds that are the remains of its foundation. Carrabassett Lumber Company bought the mill in 1900 and sawed and shipped lumber to Boston. In 1903, Drew's Mill was dismantled and rebuilt in Farmington.

Drew's Mill sat on the west bank of the Carrabassett River, opposite where the town office stands today. COURTESY OF PHILLIPS HISTORICAL SOCIETY MUSEUM

Huse Mill made birch spools and bobbins on the west bank of the Carrabassett River in Jerusalem. Its massive stone foundation can be found in the woods just to the right of the Airport Trailhead for the Narrow Gauge Pathway. R. A. Huse & Sons, which also had milling operations in Madrid and Kingfield, built the two-story mill in 1893–1894 to take advantage of Franklin & Megantic Railway's brand-new Kingfield & Dead River line. In 1900, Huse abandoned the mill, moving all its equipment to a fancy new factory in Kingfield (its dynamo generated power to light Kingfield's streets for the first time). After a fire gutted the Kingfield plant, Huse reopened its Carrabassett mill in February 1902, but it eventually moved back to Kingfield.

Lawrence Plywood Co.'s plant stood directly across the Carrabassett River from the Drew's Mill site and was the last mill to operate in the Carrabassett River Valley. Its founders were Edward Varney (a Fall River, Massachusetts, box maker) and Charles P. Hutchins and William C. Atwater (the owners of Carrabassett Timberland and Dead River Timberland companies). The mill opened in November 1923 and employed 120 men, who cut trees on Carrabassett Timberland's land in Jerusalem or made and shipped plywood packing cases to New England textile mills. "Lawrence Plywood not only never made a profit but became a rathole down which more and more capital was poured," writes Charles Hutchins's son, Curtis M. Hutchins, in *Dead River Company: A History, 1907–1972*. In 1931, Varney, who had been managing the mill, sold his stock to Dead River Timberland, which by then had absorbed its Carrabassett Timberland sister. Lawrence Plywood's new manager, Clyde Jacobs, attempted to diversify, but he had no better luck than Varney. Under Jacobs's direction, the mill sold hardwood panels to furniture makers in Massachusetts and white birch veneer to candy-stick maker Cummings Co. in Norway, Maine. It also made new S.A.W. (Strike-Anywhere) matches for Diamond Match Company's Oakland plant, but the matches didn't sell well. On May 30, 1936, Dead River liquidated Lawrence Plywood and used the mill for storage (its local manager, Ken Packard, also lived there for twenty years). The buildings fell into disrepair and were razed in 1958.

The only visible remnants are a concrete pad on the river's east bank; if anything else remains, it's under the Carrabassett Valley Town Office.

Prouty & Miller, the Newport, Vermont, company that purchased Crockertown Lumber's operation in 1902, was the largest mill to operate in the Carrabassett Valley and one of the largest in Franklin County. It covered thirty acres with a two-story mill, blacksmith shop, storehouse and general store, and manmade pond, along with two thousand acres of forestland. The company employed one hundred people, who worked around the clock, turning out thirty-five million feet of long lumber, twenty-thousand shingles, thirty thousand laths, and seven thousand clapboards in a year. Many of them lived in the boarding house or one of the two dozen or so houses clustered just south of the mill, a stone's throw from the entrance to today's Sugarloaf access road. Prouty and Miller company generated its own electricity, so the complex was illuminated at night, and it used mill waste—chips, sawdust, and shavings—to fuel its three boilers. Sometime after the Bigelow settlement was deserted, Stratton mill owner Oramendal Blanchard moved many of the houses to Blanchard Avenue in Stratton to provide housing for his workers (Kenny Wing has identified twenty-three of them that are still standing). Prouty & Miller sold its land, about two thousand acres stretching from the current location of Hug's restaurant to Bigelow Hill, to Mark H. Merrow and Leon Wardwell in 1920. In 1938, Wardwell sold out to Merrow, who died that same year. Merrow's daughters, Evelyn Brown and Mary McDonald (later Mary White), inherited the property, with Brown conveying her interest to White in 1957. For several years, White and her husband operated White's Cabins, comprising six hunting and fishing camps on Bigelow Hill. Remains of the Prouty & Miller complex can be found in the woods across Route 27 from Bigelow Station, on Sugarloaf resort property. Among the remnants are the rock foundation that supported the steam engines; scatterings of fire brick made by Scottish company Garcraig that lined the boiler; and the ruins of a dam and the pond it created, including a channel that brought wood to the mill.

Russell Brothers & Estes Company (a.k.a. Russell Remick) had a birch mill at the junction of Poplar Stream and the Carrabassett in the late 1890s. In November 1901, the company erected a portable mill in Crockertown to supply squares of birch to its Farmington box factory. As it cleared the land of trees, it moved the mill adjacent to the next stand being sawn. It was destroyed by fire in January 1906.

4

Laying Down Tracks

On July 4, 1894, conductor Ed Taylor ushered three hundred passengers aboard a train at the Kingfield depot for a celebratory ride inaugurating the F&M extension to Jerusalem. With engineer Dan Cushman at the controls and steam trailing from its chimney, Locomotive No. 1 pulled the train north, crossed over the Carrabassett's west branch, and followed newly laid tracks along the main stream's west bank for four miles. There, it crossed the Carrabassett on the iron, double-span Sanford Bridge to an area near Reed Brook called "the bluffs" (probably Reed's Falls, a.k.a. Jericho Steps). It chugged up the east bank, passing through thick woods interspersed with clearings that offered grand views of the surrounding mountains. Perhaps the riders marveled at the levelness of the valley and the straightness of the roadbed, unique in Franklin County, where, as a *Phillips Phonograph* reporter put it, other railroads had been built with "curves of a degree almost impossible in practical railroad work" and grades that would have "utterly discouraged railroad promoters with less energy and courage than the original projectors of these various enterprises possessed." This route's most significant curve was just seven degrees, and its bed ran northward on a gentle ascent, which worked in the railroad's favor because trains loaded with freight could make the ten-mile return to Kingfield using a negligible amount of steam.

The passengers debarked at Carrabassett Station, a one-and-a-half-story unpainted, rough-boarded covered depot that stood near the intersection of today's Carriage and Gauge roads. They saw evidence nearby that the railroad was already living up to its promises. In addition to

Passengers and crew at Carrabassett Station. Railroad historian Guy Rioux said the photo may depict the July 4, 1894, opening celebration of F&M's Kingfield & Dead River line. COURTESY OF PHILLIPS HISTORICAL SOCIETY MUSEUM

Grant's Mill (a.k.a. Drew's Mill), which had been manufacturing shingles on the south side of the Carrabassett River for fifteen years, the R. A. Huse company was putting finishing touches on a sprawling spool-and-bobbin mill complex just north of the station, near Huston Brook. The wings on the two-story main structure stretched the facade to eighty-seven feet. An 80-hp engine capable of cutting two thousand cords of birch a year had just been installed. In the yard, six hundred cords of logs stood ready to be sawed and shipped as soon as the railroad officially opened. The company estimated that there was enough white birch in the area to keep the mill operating for twenty years.

On August 1, the first train over the line from Strong to Carrabassett made the twenty-four-mile trip, with three stops, in just under hour. Soon after the line opened, B. D. Dyer launched a stagecoach service from Carrabassett Station to hunting-and-fishing destination Stratton. Throughout the next winter, logging contractors and mill operators from

The Carrabassett rail yard, probably prior to 1903. The Carrabassett Hotel is at left.
COURTESY OF RANGELEY LAKES REGION HISTORICAL SOCIETY

north Kingfield to Jerusalem piled huge quantities of logs and lumber beside the tracks. One K&DR passenger remarked that the entire route resembled one big lumberyard.

Before long, "Carrabassett" fell into common use for the small village that was growing around the depot, beginning with a post office and Carrabassett House and Cottages, built by railroad trustee Philip H. Stubbs to lodge the mills' visiting customers and, he hoped, sportsmen interested in trying their luck in the Carrabassett before hopping onto the stage to Stratton. In July 1897, an unnamed *Franklin Chronicle* writer stayed at the "handsome and commodious hotel, which is now leased and run by Mr. Geo. Payne and his genial wife." He and his party found Carrabassett's lumber camps and mills as entertaining as the fishing. "Only nine families reside in the township [Jerusalem], yet there is a big amount of business transacted every year," he wrote. He visited the Russell Bros.-Estes Co. mill at the junction of Poplar Stream and the Carrabassett River, where some 630,000 squares of birch were awaiting shipment to Farmington. Come September, the manager had told him, twenty-five horse teams would be hauling 130 cords per day to the mill. In addition, S. D. Warren Co. had 150 men cutting poplar for its Cumberland Mills paper factory in Westbrook, a crew was cutting one thousand cords for Jenkins-Bogart Novelty Turning Works in Kingfield, and Huse Mill was turning several hundred cords of birch into spools. It was business as usual at Grant's Mill, except for owner C. Grant Jr.'s side project: he was building a flying machine. "[It] is stored in the attic of his mill, so it is said, and he is very secret in his work—nobody except himself sees or works upon it."

Though clearly a boon for lumbering, the F&M had been just scraping by, barely posting a profit some years, running a deficit others. By 1897, the F&M's bonds had been in default all of its thirteen years, and the Kingfield–Carrabassett extension for three and a half years. The railroad's bondholders voted to foreclose each mortgage and take possession of the company. The following year, the reorganized Franklin & Megantic Railway was sold to the Sandy River Railroad Co. for $87,000 in stock.

A locomotive leaves a train shed that was located near the site of today's town office.
COURTESY OF GUY RIOUX

Waiting for the train in Carrabassett. COURTESY OF GUY RIOUX

Despite the tenuous finances, the railroad grew. In September 1898, the track was extended about four thousand feet north of Carrabassett Station to serve the S. D. Warren logging site, which was shipping fifteen to twenty thousand cords of pulpwood a year to the Westbrook mill. Then, in September 1899, a ninety-man rail gang began building a seven-mile extension to Crockertown, which had just been purchased for $110,000 by Frank Barnjum's newly formed Crockertown Lumber Company. The company had erected two portable mills near the future terminus, each capable of processing twenty-five thousand board feet a day, and two hundred axe-men were in the woods chopping spruce, birch, and poplar.[14] It was "the most extensive lumbering operation ever seen in this section," according to the *Phillips Phonograph*. Carrabassett Station agent H. O. Lisherness told the newspaper that twelve tons of grain and provisions arrived at the depot every day to supply the logging and rail-gang camps.

That upbeat news was overshadowed by a *Boston Globe* front-page interview with two men, Thomas Macullar and Edward Kearney, who claimed to have fled from the railroad gang after working under cruel conditions. Macullar spoke in a hoarse whisper, the symptom of a nasty

14. Barnjum also erected a portable mill at Hammond Field around the same time.

A train crosses the trestle in Carrabassett. The bridge now supports Ted Jones's driveway, opposite 1121 Carrabassett Drive. COURTESY OF GUY RIOUX

cold he blamed on the crew's sleeping quarters: a leaky twenty-seven-by-thirty-foot camp. He testified that workers, some clothed only in their underwear, had been made to labor in cold rain and mud for twelve hours. The contractor, William B. Smith, "abuses nearly every one of the men," Macullar went on. He recounted shoveling by the roadbed, when Smith approached and yelled at him for not working hard enough. Smith threatened to shoot him if he didn't pick up the pace. Another afternoon, a different boss beat a worker black and blue for not walking fast enough while carrying picks and shovels up a mountainside.

"Smith has four scouts in the woods, and their duty is to see that none of the laborers escape," the *Globe* charged. "Macullar and Kearney broke away from the camp at 2 o'clock in the morning, and went through the woods until they reached a railroad, and then made their way to Portland and came to Boston by boat. They said they were rightly glad to get away from the camp and allow Smith the money due them for the work they had done during the week." They were owed $1.50 apiece for each day worked, as well as their board and fare to Carrabassett.

Teacher Julia Small with her class at the Carrabassett School House in 1927–1928.
COURTESY OF JAY AND WENDY WYMAN

Ever a champion of railroad and lumbering interests, the *Phonograph* called Macullar and Kearney's claims "misleading to say the least" and a "slur on the reputation of Contractor Smith." The journal's source was Smith's bookkeeper, who said his boss had never before been accused of abuse and who described Macullar and Kearney as unskilled and lazy. "Macullar was no good at all, although he was not afraid of work, being able to lie down and go to sleep beside it," the *Phonograph* harrumphed. Their boss came off as stoic. "Smith is now pushing matters on the road and has about a hundred men at work. He has the road graded for 3½ miles above Carrabassett and has a crew now at work laying iron and sleepers [ties]."

When railroads were being built and logging operations were going full tilt, Maine contractors often couldn't find enough local help, so they turned to employment agencies to meet the need for section hands and lumberjacks. Macullar and Kearney were just two of scores of out-of-staters who, like the Italians, were lured to the Jerusalem by hiring agents rhapsodizing about the pleasures of working outdoors—how the sun in a man's face and the fresh air in his lungs would make him fit and clear his mind. The recruits came in such numbers that the F&M ran special "lumberjack trains" that pulled four or five jam-packed passenger cars to the worksites. They were often barely qualified. "Sometimes the men would arrive in low shoes and street clothes," Herschel Boyton, an F&M engineer, told Robert C. Jones, the author of the 1979 history *Two Feet between the Rails.* "Sometimes the company would provide appropriate clothings and an axe; then the man would be on his own. He was paid by the cord. It is said that a good many left the job without having cut enough timber to even cover their bills at the boardinghouse." In 1907, in fact, such harsh labor practices were legalized when lumber barons persuaded Maine legislators to adopt a peonage law modeled after Alabama's. More than three hundred men throughout the state, many of them hired under false pretenses, were jailed for quitting their jobs. The law was repealed in 1917.

Nothing came of Macullar and Kearney's complaints. The F&M crew finished the job just before New Year's Day, and then they boarded the train and went home. The new railroad station—and the small settlement that sprouted around it—took its name from the massive mountain ridge looming over their backyard: Bigelow.

Sandy River and Rangeley Lakes No. 3, pictured between Carrabassett and Bigelow stations. COURTESY OF JAY AND WENDY WYMAN

"HOW WE LOVED THE RAILROAD!"

Permanent railroad jobs were far more appreciated than those building roadbeds and laying track, judging from Jones's interviews with former employees and their families. Cliff Cushman, a brakeman on the Sandy River Railroad, hailed from a railroading family. His father, Mel, was an SR conductor; his uncle, Dan, was the F&M's lead engineer; and Dan's brother-in-law, Elmer Voter, was an F&M brakeman. "It was a pretty good way to make a living," Cliff said. "Each day the work was a little different. Unexpected things frequently happened, and no two runs were ever exactly the same."

Hard work, long hours, and the public's high regard for the service combined to create camaraderie among the F&M crew. In 1900, they built a hunting camp two miles south of Bigelow Station, a retreat that they and their families could use free of charge (the cabin, "Riverside 1900," is still standing on the north bank of the Carrabassett and is privately owned). "On a weekend, the men would get permission from the

1905

County officials today viewed the skeleton of the man discovered by a party of fishermen in the woods two miles above Carrabassett but will not decide about holding an inquest until tomorrow. Dr. E. L. Pennell of Kingfield, who examined the bones, said the skull is not fractured. The upper jaw is in good shape, except one tooth is missing, but the lower jaw was not found. The skeleton is that of a man six feet in height. Two theories have been advanced as to the identity of the man—that he was a river driver, who disappeared three years ago and probably became lost and died from exhaustion, or was the Eustis citizen who escaped from the state insane asylum at Augusta four years ago. The clothing, except for the boots, a small piece of woolen shirt, and a portion of a pair of trousers had rotted away. —*Bangor Daily News*, July 5

officials to take an engine and coach to transport themselves and their materials to the site of the project," Arthur French, the son of engineer Charles French, told Jones. "During deer season, arrangements were frequently made to take hunting parties up to the camp in this manner. In the last years of operations, a rail bus was used. One year, no less than 16 employees were using the camp at one time. The camp proved to be one of the area's best locations for blueberrying. Often employees and their families would use the camp for vacations."

Among them was Dan Cushman's family, who went every fall. "Usually we invited another family to accompany us," writes Cushman's daughter, Hazel Cushman Erickson, in her 1971 memoir, *I Grew Up with the Narrow Gauge*. "This vacation always took place in blueberry season. . . . My mother made the most delicious blueberry pie I shall ever eat. She always made a few extra, all hot and juicy, to give to the train men as they went by the cottage."

No doubt such kindnesses were appreciated. Railroading was physically demanding, and the monetary rewards were few. The F&M offered no paid vacations, no sick leave, and no retirement benefits. Employees worked twelve hours a day, six days a week, holidays included. Cushman was often roused in the night to transport Dr. Charles Bell, the F&M company doctor, to Bigelow to tend to an injured worker or deliver a baby. They'd take an engine, just the two of them, with Dr. Bell acting as fireman, shoveling coal into the boiler's firebox. Likewise, conductors like Bill Corson did far more than punch tickets. In addition to overseeing the loading and unloading cargo, Corson was known to climb atop the coal pile at the coal dock below Bigelow Station and shovel the black rocks down to his crew mates, who in turn threw them into the coal car. Section men, meanwhile, worked year-round maintaining and repairing track. In spring, they replaced rails that had buckled and heaved in the thaw. In summer and fall, they resurfaced the entire roadbed with gravel. In winter, they shoveled snow from yards, station platforms and roofs, and—if the snowplows couldn't move—miles of track. None of these circumstances diminished employees' affections for the F&M. "How we loved the railroad!" Agnes McMullen, wife of conductor Rob McMullen, reminisced.

"[It] was awfully good to us. There will never be another like it. Many of us cried when it was done."

Weather continually tossed obstacles in the way of trains and lumbering and mill operations. In 1898, choppers were unable to work most of February, as one storm after another buried Carrabassett in seven feet of snow. The winter of 1900—the first for the Bigelow extension—was another doozy. In February, a massive snowstorm shut down the F&M. Heavy drifting and ice derailed the snowplow train in Strong, and it took several hours to get it back on track. The line between Carrabassett and Bigelow was blocked for nearly a month. Charles French left on what was to be a sixty-two-mile round-trip run of Kingfield, Bigelow, and Strong, and he didn't get home for three weeks. A month later, heavy rain followed by freezing temperatures turned floodwaters into a solid mass of ice. Then came a big snowstorm, burying the tracks under four feet of ice and snow. "That was a horrible winter," French said.

Hazel Cushman Erickson, daughter of engineer Dan Cushman, described the jaunt to Bigelow as perilous: "On one side, as high up as one could see, was a ledge which seemed to reach the sky. On the other side, down, down, a long way down, was the rocky Carrabassett River, flowing gently in summer, but turbulent, foaming, gushing over rocks in spring, and at times jammed by ice floes piled up and crested nearly to the railroad's edge. The danger here was the undermining of the rails." In severe weather, Erickson's father would slow the train to a creep. Even so, he was involved in seven tip-overs, the first one in driving rain.

Summer brought its own set of challenges. In 1900—a tough year all around, it seems—drought forced some river-powered mills to shut down. Trains throwing sparks ignited several fires. One blaze turned fifteen hundred cords of S. D. Warren's peeled poplar to ash. In the heat, rails popped out of ties along a long section of track.

Whether started by trains spewing cinders, faulty sawmill engines, or careless campers and sportsmen, fires were an ever-present danger. Many mills burned down, including those owned by Crockertown Lumber and its Bigelow successor, Prouty & Miller, both of which were quickly rebuilt.

A blaze in the drought-ridden summer of 1908—the third-worst fire season since Maine started keeping records in 1903—may have hastened the decline of mills in the Carrabassett River Valley region.[15] "Sunday a serious fire broke out on the timberland owned by the Great Northern Paper company," the Phillips-based *Maine Woods* newspaper reported on June 19. "The timely rainfall of Tuesday put an end to the fire, but not until it had burned over about 2,000 acres of cut-over land. . . . There also were destroyed several hundred cords of pulp wood ready for market. Two lumber camps were also destroyed. The paper company sent a crew of 40 men, and Fire Warden Frank Savage had 75 more who took turns fighting the flames. The smoke could be seen for miles, and the blaze at one time threatened to spread over a vast territory of valuable timberlands."

In fact, the fire of 1908, probably started by a train, burned more than twice the acreage reported in that initial account. It started at Hammond Field, a log landing served by a railroad spur that came across the river. It spread over Hammond Pond Mountain—henceforth known as Burnt Mountain—and then across the north side of Sugarloaf and west of Caribou Pond Road to Crocker Mountain.[16] The flames came within a half mile of Bigelow, where a train was standing by to evacuate residents.

1897

Burglars broke into the post office at Carrabassett Wednesday night but not finding anything they climbed on the roof of the plaza and made an entrance to the sleeping room of the proprietor of the Carrabassett House where they secured about $400. They made their escape and are still at large. Officers are looking for them. —*Franklin Chronicle*, September 9

---

15. Fires across the state that year destroyed an estimated 142,310 acres of timberland, valued at $618,816 (the equivalent of $17.8 million in 2021). The next year, the Maine Forestry District was established to protect nearly ten million acres in the state's northern unorganized townships.

16. While the damage was extensive, this fire resulted in the terrain that provides some of the above-treeline skiing on Sugarloaf today.

The week the blaze broke out, a crew from the Yale School of Forestry had been surveying the land to develop conservation harvesting practices for its new owner, Carrabassett Timberland Company. Founded by New York–based coal dealer William C. Atwater and Atwater's partner and New England sales representative, Charles P. Hutchins, Carrabassett Timberland had just purchased most of Frank Barnjum's Jerusalem holdings, about sixteen thousand acres, in order to supply spruce to its cash-strapped partner, Great Northern Paper Company. "The fire was the beginning of the demise of the mills along the Carrabassett River because it burned so much wood," Kenny Wing believes. "Mills would only last as long as the wood supply."

Still, there were plenty of trees to keep them going for a while. Great Northern Paper Company owned about twenty thousand acres in Bigelow and Wyman Township, which it had acquired from Prouty & Miller Lumber Co. in 1905. Prouty & Miller, which had purchased that land from Barnjum, retained about two thousand acres and a large mill complex opposite Bigelow Station. In 1909, Atwater and Hutchins formed a new corporation called the Dead River Timberland Co., which purchased what is today Alder Stream Township and eventually absorbed Carrabassett Timberland. Dead River would grow to become one of Maine's largest and most diversified businesses, with interests in everything from building supplies to lobstering to film processing—as well as the Carrabassett River Valley's longest continuously operating timberland owner.

1930

Government engineers, surveying the Stratton and Phillips Quadranges, have found two mountains in that section that overtop Bigelow's 4,150 feet. Sugarloaf Mountain, in Crocker, 4,237 feet high, is the second highest mountain in the state, and Crockertown Mountain, 4,168 feet, is the third highest, their measurements show. Mount Katahdin, with a summit 5,268 feet above mean sea level, is the highest peak in Maine.
—*Bangor Daily News*, August 27

By 1916, Bigelow was no longer a busy lumbering center, and the railroad continued to struggle. The Maine Public Utilities Commission approved the closure of the Carrabassett-to-Bigelow line, though only 3,103 feet of siding was abandoned at that time. The track was finally removed in July and August 1927, the same year that state highway Route 27 was built to replace the old county road. Linking Kingfield and Eustis, the new highway made it easier for sportsmen to visit—and for trucks to transport lumber. Building mills close to timberlands and track was no longer a big advantage for lumber companies. When the F&M shut down in 1932, only one mill, Lawrence Plywood, was still operating in the valley. Its owner, Dead River Timberland, successfully petitioned the railroad commission to reopen the F&M, but the reprieve lasted less than two years as the demand for plywood evaporated. Dead River closed the mill in 1936, leaving the twenty families who resided in Carrabassett without steady employment.

In 1938, Ken Packard arrived in the valley to run a Dead River Company lumber camp and took up residence in the mill's office, where he lived for twenty years.[17] What remained of the former settlement were vacant and neglected buildings that eventually collapsed or succumbed to fire. "By 1944, all that was left in the valley was the old mill, which was used for storage for Dead River's supplies," Laura Dunham wrote in the *Sugarloaf Irregular* (now the *Irregular*). "Finally, the roof caved in, and it became necessary to destroy the mill in 1958; the last dreams of what used to be a thriving town."

From the distance of a century, the logging-railroad era is but a blip on the Carrabassett timeline, but it established the infrastructure for what was to come. To those whose livelihoods depended on it, the F&M was a lifetime, and its demise unfolded slowly, as the highway that ran beside the track filled with trucks and cars. "They started cutting off trains, and finally, I didn't have a regular job," Cliff Cushman said. "It was hard to leave the railroad and find steady work elsewhere. It was a great bunch of fellows to work with. We worked awfully hard, but I never had a job I enjoyed more than railroading."

---

17. In 1956, Packard built a house in a birch grove on the Carrabassett's east bank, a landmark because of its own private bridge to Route 27. The house is today owned by Ted Jones.

Interlude

BIGELOW STATION

Bigelow Station's life as a railroad depot was short. Completed in the summer of 1901, it served lumber mills and travelers for just twenty-six years. Sportsmen and skiers have made it their camp for far longer—nearly a century—and yet, as of 2022, most of its original details (including ticket windows, kerosine heater, and a wall-mounted, hand-crank telephone) survived. It's the oldest building in town.

Credit for preserving the station goes to the Bell and Folger families, who have owned it since the mid-1950s. Annie Bell, the widow of

Bigelow Station circa 1940. COURTESY OF GUY RIOUX

F&M company doctor Charles Bell, purchased the station, a freight shed, and land for $1 from a Eustis couple, Robert and Priscilla Lindstrom. Later, she gave the station to her nephew, Philip "Brud" Folger, as a wedding present.

In the 1950s and 1960s, the area was off the electrical grid, and the station had no generator and no improvements of any kind. For water, the Folgers went down to the river with pails. They have since added modern living quarters at the rear of the building, but the original station's interior and exterior are much as they were when the F&M was in business.

The station sits in the center of a cluster of small camps dating to Sugarloaf's beginnings and earlier. One of the oldest is Howard Ross's Brookside Cabin, the log structure that practically juts into Route 27. Ross's grandfather, Arthur Ross, built it when Route 27 was still a carriage road. When the road was expanded to three lanes on Bigelow Hill in the 1960s, a survey revealed that a corner of Brookside's bunk room poked into the state's right-of-way. Arthur Ross also built the cabin next door to Brookside.

Before Annie Bell purchased Bigelow Station, her son, Farmington insurance agent and Sugarloaf Mountain Corporation board member Dick Bell, bought an adjacent parcel and cabin. There, he built the ski camp that still bears the name he gave it: Sno-dunder. At the time, his neighbors were brothers Jonathan, Roger, and Norton Luce, who'd purchased their own log cabin in 1956 from Thomas Slattery of Minot. The Luces' deed specified that Stratton fur trapper Gust Johnson retained the right to a shed on the property "for his own use as long as he lives." In 1963, Bell bought and razed the Luces' cabin, as well as the cabin next to Sno-dunder, and moved a Farmington diner kitchen to the site and converted it to a camp. After Johnson's death, Bell sold the lot containing the shed. Today, Nick Karahalios owns Bell's transplanted camp, and Dick Bell's daughter, Elizabeth "Buffy" Bell-Folsom, owns Sno-dunder.

It was Bell who convinced his mother to buy Bigelow Station. "As a kid, she'd ridden on the first railroad train that ever went into Strong," Folger said. "The engine was pushing a flat car, and she was on it. She also rode on the last train that ever left Strong. She had an enthusiasm for the trains, and she was interested in what her kids and grandkids were doing—everyone was skiing at Sugarloaf."

An early member of the Sugarloaf board of directors, Richard Bell was introduced to the area through his job selling insurance in the 1950s. "Many times I would ride with him," Folger said. "He was a good friend of [Sugarloaf founder] Amos Winter, and we would always stop and see him in his store in Kingfield."

5

Making Sport

Within three years of the K&DR's 1894 inaugural run to Carrabassett, lumbering operations were creeping northward in search of
unbroken timberlands, and the little settlement around the depot was
becoming known as both a gateway to the legendary Dead River sporting
camps and a hunting-and-fishing destination in its own right. Fueled by
a nationwide back-to-nature movement that was then at its height, the

This Route 27 camp is the only surviving cottage of Carrabassett Spring
Farm, a turn-of-the-twentieth-century health retreat. Locals call it the
Crow's Nest, but historian Kenny Wing says the moniker originally
applied to a neighboring dwelling that was razed. AUTHOR

reputation would outlast the railroad and the mills and serve as a bridge to the recreation-based culture and economy that has come to define the town of Carrabassett Valley.

Turn-of-the-twentieth-century tenderfoots living in polluted, over-crowded cities counted among their heroes Teddy Roosevelt, who'd cut his hunting teeth in the Maine north woods, and Joseph Knowles, who captivated a national audience in the summer of 1913 when, naked and without tools, he entered the wilderness north of Bigelow to prove he could survive for two months on his wits and skills alone (in fact, Knowles spent most of the time drinking beer in a cabin with a female companion, according to a Stratton wilderness guide paid to help him with the fak-ery). The Dead River region, the *Maine Woodsman* wrote, beckoned "the overwrought merchant, capitalist, manufacturer, the worn lawyer, weary doctor, clergyman, and scholar," who were looking to awaken their inner frontiersman, if only for a few days a year.

Among those who visited Jerusalem in August 1897 was a party from New York City who rented a riverside farmhouse about one mile south of Carrabassett Station. By the end of their stay, one of the city slickers swore that the pure, cold water he'd been drinking from a nearby spring

Spring Farm Hotel as seen from the north side of the Carrabassett River. Route 27 passes through the spot where the barn stood. COURTESY OF ALLAN SOCEA

A Record's Camps guest tries his luck at Poplar Stream Falls.

had cured the constipation he'd suffered for years despite remedies recommended by his doctors in the United States and Europe.

That claim was music to the ears of Boston businessman and Jerusalem landowner Charles G. Smith, who believed his own chronic ailments had been relieved by his daily consumption of that same spring water. Smith saw an opportunity to merge gunning vacations with another back-to-nature trend: water-cure getaways, which were being marketed to wealthy urbanites suffering from the ill effects of exhausting work schedules and indulgent diets. Mineral springs were often viewed as healing potions, and people would journey for miles to "take the waters" at spas like Poland Spring in southwest Maine.

Smith purchased the farmhouse, the spring, and the twenty mostly cleared acres on which they sat. He built cottages on both sides of the river, connecting them with a pretty foot bridge. For the first few years, his spa, Carrabassett Spring Farm, had the added attraction of a "game park"—really just a fenced area populated with two black bears, two buffaloes, two elks, and several white-tail deer.[18] Between that and the mineral spring, Carrabassett Spring Farm was the most colorful and most publicized accommodation in the valley during the rail era—popular enough to have its own depot. "Step from the cars right at the door of a hotel and comfortable cabins and find the best fishing close at hand," a newspaper ad enticed in 1899. "Wild deer can be seen quite often from the house, and the hunter does not have to buckboard or stage. A very objectionable feature to many elderly people, those who are not strong, and ladies is the many miles of staging and buckboarding, which they are obliged to take at many places. Here it is avoided. Ladies can accompany their husbands, and hunt, fish, and rest as they please."[19] A week's stay at Carrabassett Spring Farm, which was open year-round, cost $8–$12 (the equivalent of $242–$364 in 2021).

---

18. The Stanley Museum in Kingfield has two Carrabassett Mineral Spring Farm postcards, one showing two buffalo named Admiral and Maude, the other a bear cub named Dinah. "Many Maine communities at this time had bounties on adult bears, which could sometimes result in orphaned bear cubs," according to the Maine Historical Society's Maine Memory Network.

19. A horse-drawn buckboard is little more than a plank with a seat stretched between the front and rear axles. "It was the crudest form of a carriage," Kenny Wing said. "When you have wooden spoke rims with iron rims on it, there's no suspension. It was just boards and the boards bucked. Holy Jesus, does it ride rough."

Owen Fenderson, nephew of Record's Camps owners Valerie and Ralph Gould, with his dog, Billie, in 1944. The photographer was likely standing about where Ayotte's store is today. The Coca-Cola sign sits on the future site of Sugarloaf Airport.
COURTESY OF SUSAN HARRISON

Sept 7, 1936
Record's Store Carrabasset Maine

Record's Store in 1936. COURTESY OF JAY AND WENDY WYMAN

Other publicity that same year suggests that Carrabassett House, the hotel built by railroad trustee Phillip Stubbs and leased by Dr. George Payne and his wife, shared the game park with Spring Farm. An *Oxford Democrat* correspondent who stopped at Carrabassett House on a June 1899 railroad tour of Franklin County enthused about the hotel's native buffaloes, elk, and deer. The *Phillips Phonograph* likewise remarked on Payne's penned animals. Once, after searchers found and returned his escaped doe, Payne awoke the next morning to find two does in his enclosure. "For the life of him, he could not distinguish the wild deer from the tame one," the *Phonograph* wrote. Not knowing which animal to release, Payne asked Maine Inland Fish and Game for permission to keep the interloper. The department's commissioners consented, provided the doctor compensate the state. Payne replied that he didn't care to pay for the deer, and if the state wanted its property, it should come to the game park and get it—just don't confuse it with his deer. The commissioners gave in, and Payne kept both deer.

Camp Red Dog, one of Record's cabins, in 1920.
COURTESY OF JAY AND WENDY WYMAN

Payne promoted the spring water as if he had a share in the business, though his name didn't appear among the principals when Smith and four partners incorporated Carrabassett Mineral Spring Co. in 1902. One of dozens of commercial springs in Maine at the time, the company bottled water at the farm and shipped it by train to Boston, where it was sold as "fine table water" and a cure for bladder and kidney diseases, constipation, diabetes, dyspepsia "in all its forms," edema, fevers, indigestion, gout, and "torpid liver," a common turn-of-the-twentieth-century diagnosis for pretty much any vague malady. Payne went even further in touting the spring water as a curative, saying it had made his guests "well and strong." In an article for the *Phillips Phonograph*, he boasted that "the water is of excellent medicinal virtue, having a specific action on the kidneys and bladder, disease of which yields rapidly to its action. I wish to call to the attention of the medical profession the special action upon

1898

George Woodcock, of Carrabasset, shot a doe deer last Saturday on Stratton Brook that had a well-developed set of spike horns. Another hunter, Edward Taylor, shot the fawn that was with the doe. Aside from the horns, the deer was exactly like any other doe, and weighed 125 pounds. —*Forest and Stream*, December 31

specific diseases that this water has. Except the hot springs of Arkansas, I have never found its equal in nearly 30 years of practice both externally and internally. In time, I believe that many sufferers will find their way to this section for that relief that no other place in New England can give." His hotel, he added, had been overcrowded that week with doctors, judges, and professors from Boston, Chicago, New York, and even Paris (Paris, Kentucky, that is).

ABUNDANT GAME AND EXCESSIVE HUNTING

The city dwellers who came to Maine to hunt may have fancied themselves sportsmen in the Teddy Roosevelt mold, but a significant number disregarded his calls for conservation-minded hunting and fishing. To be sure, Maine had plenty of homegrown poachers, some of them dangerous men, but the wasteful slaughter of game animals was almost exclusively the domain of urbanites "from away." They had a reputation across the state for killing far more moose, deer, and caribou than they could eat, never mind transport home on a train.[20] Some would kill an animal just for a head mount, leaving the rest of the body to rot in the woods. Others didn't even bother to take a trophy.

---

20. Unscrupulous hunters are partly to blame for decimating Maine's once-abundant caribou herd. In 1899, the state placed a six-year ban on hunting caribou, but the population didn't recover. Loss of habitat due to timber harvesting and farming also contributed to the population's decline. The last caribou sighting in Maine was near Katahdin in 1914.

1898

Word has been received that a special fish car will be here, under the charge of Mr. J.B. Rogers, messenger of the U.S. Fish commission, with a carload of trout and salmon to be distributed among the different bodies of water in the Dead River region. This is good news, and preparations for transporting the fish north from Farmington are being made. The young fish will go in by way of Carrabassett and will be taken in charge by special teams at that station, which is the end of the railroad in that direction. —*Boston Globe*, October 30

"One can understand a person killing for food, but to indiscriminately kill for the sake of killing is quite beyond comprehension," the *Maine Woodsman* editorialized. "Still, there is a class of men who kill for just the reason that it is lawful to kill. They'll fish a stream to death in the season, not because they want the fish, but because they can. It is this class of people who force the legislature to enact laws that interfere with the greatest enjoyment of the true hunter."

With bag limits, seasons, and prohibitions on practices like crust hunting (shooting large animals struggling to walk on crusted snow), the state strove to get control of the phenomenon while still encouraging a lucrative and growing recreational activity. "The constant increase in the number of sportsmen who come to Maine each year to spend their vacations in hunting and fishing conclusively demonstrates the wisdom of protecting and preserving the fish and game of our state and is a sufficient warrant for the large sums of money which have been expended for that purpose," Governor John F. Hill said in his January 1901 inaugural address. "The past season has been the most successful one in the history of our fish and game interests. Including the amount paid transportation companies, it is estimated that during the year 1900 at least $5 million was expended by more than 50,000 visitors to our forests and inland lakes."

1908

Carrabasset Spring, belonging to the Carrabasset Mineral Spring Water Company, of Boston, is situated on the bank of a small stream 10 feet above water level, on the Franklin and Megantic Railway, a short distance south of Carrabasset Station. It issues near the base of a sand plain which rises only 10 feet higher at its central point, about 250 feet away. The spring was formed by digging a well 15 feet deep to a soft, shale-like rock. The water is reported to come from the rock. It is colorless, odorless, and tasteless, and has a temperature reported to be 46 degrees in summer and 42 degrees in winter. The flow is 5 gallons a minute after a storm and 2½ gallons a minute during a dry spell. It is said that after a heavy rain an hour or so elapses before the spring is affected. The water is used for drinking at a farm and two cottages situated nearby and is bottled and shipped to Boston as a table and medicinal water. The price is 25 cents a gallon, or $1 for a 5-gallon bottle. A part of the water is carbonated. The company runs a bottling establishment on the spot, and the spring is well protected by curbing on all sides.
—*Underground Waters of Southern Maine*, Department of Interior, United States Geological Survey

In 1903, the state began requiring nonresidents to purchase a hunting license, a move supported by the *Maine Woodsman*, even if it meant a temporary drop in visitors to the Dead River region. "It might be a good thing to have the number diminished for one year so as to give the game a chance to gain somewhat on the drain annually growing heavier and heavier, although of course it is most desirable to have their money for the warden service."

The newspaper offered no examples of wanton slaughter specific to Carrabassett and Bigelow, but the numbers of animals routinely (and legally) taken there are excessive by twenty-first-century standards, which limit each hunter to one deer per season and each fisherman to two brook trout and one landlocked salmon per day. Consider the *Boston Globe's* report from Carrabassett on May 16, 1897: "The best catch of brook trout yet was made by Messrs Harvey Harlow and J. H. Myers, who in four hours caught 380 trout on the Carrabassett." Likewise, a *Farmington Chronicle* correspondent who spent a couple nights at Carrabassett House boasted that he and his friends "secured several hundred nice brook trout" during a single day of fishing at Redington and Poplar streams. In July 1900, the *Phillips Phonograph* celebrated the excellent trout fishing season underway in Carrabassett: "Raymond Phillips of Kingfield yanked out 50 last Thursday, and they were good ones too. Conductor Corson of the Franklin & Megantic railroad frequently goes down while waiting and gets a mess of the speckled beauties. Six men from here have taken from the river over 700 trout this season."

Hunters, too, took game in large numbers. Typical of the news reports coming out of Carrabassett is one congratulating two Oxford County sportsmen who bagged four deer in just four hours and another

White's Cabins on Bigelow Hill, probably in the late 1950s or early 1960s. The flip side of this postcard reads, "Bigelow Village at the foot of Sugarloaf Mountain . . . Duplex Cottages with Kitchenettes . . . Unexcelled Skiing, Hunting and Fishing."
COURTESY OF JAY AND WENDY WYMAN

1919

The day was devoted to a long trip through the valley of the Carrabassett River, across Jerusalem, to Dead River, Flagstaff, Eustis, and southward around the western end of Mt. Bigelow through Coplin and Crockertown.... At bog pond in Jerusalem were found *Scheuchzeria palustris, Eriophorum callitrix, Carex limosa,* and *Habenaria blephariglottis.* Here *Nuphar rubrodisca* was conspicuous by its depauperate size and scarcity, while the margin of the pond was brilliant with horned bladderwort. —Minutes of the Kingfield Meeting, July 9, Josselyn Botanical Society of Maine

(Common names in order are pod grass, arctic cottongrass, mud sedge, white fringed orchid, water lily, and horned bladderwort.)

about a Massachusetts hunting party that shipped fifteen bucks and does over the F&M.[21] The F&M crew was known for hunting deer not only from the train but also *with* the train. "Countless deer were killed by passing trains—both intentionally and unintentionally," Arthur French related in *Two Feet between the Rails.* "A good many trains came back into Kingfield where a deer that had been struck was quickly dressed in the roundhouse. One of the engineers built up a particularly impressive record of bagging deer with his engine. He would slow his train down until the deer would decide to cross the tracks; then he would open the throttle—often with the desired results.... Quite a number of the employees were able to reduce their family meat bills in this somewhat unconventional and illegal manner."

The railroad and its friends in the press were the biggest champions of the Carrabassett River Valley as a vacation destination, so when the F&M shut down in 1932, promotion of the area pretty much ended. The atmosphere of hopeful, heady growth evaporated, and the sportsmen who

---

21. Today, Maine law prohibits doe hunting except by special permit during both the firearms and the muzzleloader seasons. The permits are issued by lottery.

still came liked it that way. Some of them built cabins on lots leased from the state. Others stayed at housekeeping cottages like Record's Camps (which were located along the west bank of the Carrabassett just north of today's Sugarloaf Regional Airport) and White's Cabins (located on Bigelow Hill on former Prouty & Miller land). Carrabassett Spring Farm's main building was destroyed by a chimney fire in May 1913, but its six cabins and barn were saved. The resort operated for a couple more decades, though water cures were no longer the draw. The perceived medicinal value of mineral water had declined with the discovery of antibiotics like penicillin and the introduction of industrial bottling, which made the product commonplace. Through the 1940s and 1950s, the Carrabassett River Valley was an unsung sporting paradise, a quiet alternative to Stratton, Rangeley, and Moosehead Lake, known only to a few.

Record's Camps:
A Bridge between Two Eras

Record's Camps, a hunting retreat with six log cabins and a store called the Oasis, was one of the few railroad-era businesses still operating when Amos Winter and the Bigelow Boys began cutting trails on Sugarloaf Mountain in 1952.

William Record, a former Portland Railroad motorman and Forster Manufacturing Co. millworker, purchased a seventy-five-acre field in Jerusalem Township in 1912. With his second wife, Edith, and his brothers, James and Frank, Record built a two-story house with ell. He also built the cabins, spacing them widely along the edge of the field, where Huse Mill Road is today (the mill had been closed for ten years by the time the Records arrived). The Oasis sat alongside the dirt road that would become Route 27—in fact, its single gas pump was in the street. A sign reading "HOT DOGS and SANDWICHES" hung over a wrap-around porch furnished with a few tables and chairs. The cabins and store were seasonal. William and Edith spent winters in Orland, California, where they had a cottage and orange grove.

After Edith's death in 1921, William's oldest daughter, Valerie, and her husband, Ralph Gould, helped him run the camps. In 1934, they took in their nephew, one-year-old Owen, after his mother, Irene Record Fenderson, had been suddenly widowed and had to work outside the home. Owen rode the stagecoach to and from school in Stratton. Valerie cared for him until he was a teenager, when he went back to live with his mother in Oakland.

Not long before his death in 1940, William Record gave a one-hundred-square-foot parcel to his nephews, Otho and Clyde Record, who moved the former Bigelow schoolhouse there. Today Owen Fenderson's children use the schoolhouse as a camp. It sits on the east side of the airport.

Valerie and Ralph Gould inherited the rest of the property and gave a one-acre lot and cabin to Irene, who lived there with her second husband, Harry Ware. Irene worked for both Leo Tague and Ma Judson, making her a familiar face to Sugarloaf regulars in the 1960s.

The Wares' cabin was destroyed by a fire years ago. In 1956, Ralph Gould, by then a widower, sold Record's Camps to the Tague family.

Interlude
THE MYSTERY OF CAMP RUIN

John and Ann van C. Parker, Scott Scully, Bill Poole, John Robinson, Alice Mary Pierce, and "Woolly" and Hoddy Hildreth rented the former sawmill bunk house they called "Camp Ruin" for the first time in the winter of 1959–1960. What follows is an abbreviated version of a tale that John van Parker shared with the Carrabassett Valley History Committee before his death in 2018. His story was originally published in the Sugarloaf Ski Club newsletter.

In the mid-1960s, three wood-frame buildings stood diagonally across Route 27 from Bigelow Station. They were affectionately called Camp Bruin (because lessee Parker Poole killed a bear nearby), Camp Ruin, and Camp Scr—(also known as the Infirmary). They had been bunkhouses for Prouty & Miller's steam-powered mill that stood at the end of the narrow-gauge railroad. Three groups of friends rented the buildings each winter for ski houses, making minimum improvements. Their heat came from wood stoves, their water was pulled through the ice of the Carrabassett River, and their facilities were outhouses. (Some of us kept portable toilet seats on the wall near the stove for cozy use when needed.)

One winter, Alice Mary Pierce, a regular member of Camp Ruin, broke her leg, and her cast was generously autographed and illustrated. After it was removed, the cast became a key decoration for the camp living room. The following fall, when we made our annual trip to shovel out the outhouse, patch the tar-paper roof, and fumigate the camp for flies, we discovered the cast was missing.

Speculation as to the fate of Alice Mary's cast abounded. Eventually, someone reported that the cast had been attached to a wooden post at the corner of the bar at Chateau des Tagues. At least it was still being used as a decorative piece, and its elevation to such a conspicuous location was a source of pride. But honor dictated that it should be retrieved.

One Saturday evening, during the usual lengthy cocktail hour and into dinner, a lively conversation developed a plan to conduct an all-forces raid to retrieve the cast. After dinner, twelve of us piled into our cars and headed for Valley Crossing.

Chateau des Tagues was in full swing. There was live music, and it was standing room only. Jack Pierce and I wedged our way through the bar crowd and maneuvered to the post to which the cast was attached by wire. The rest of our team blended into the crowd and took whatever action was appropriate to divert the attention of the bartenders and waitresses.

Neither Jack nor I took off our coats. Jack's was loose-fitting and suited to the task. We untwisted the wires little by little each moment we were confident that neither a bartender nor a waitress was looking our way. After a while, Jack said, "The only thing that's holding the cast up is me." I promptly paid our bar bill and said, "Let's go."

Jack slid the cast under his coat as easily as if he were pocketing a breast wallet. We calmly walked through the crowd. The evening concluded with many toasts to Alice Mary's cast in the Camp Ruin living room.

Near the end of the season, a consensus grew that we could do better than a cast for a living room decoration, and the cast was moved to the outhouse. A few weeks later, we concluded the cast should go. During an April snowstorm, one of us hurled it track-meet hammer style toward the woods beyond the parking lot.

The next season, several of us elected to take a sauna following a hard day of skiing. We were assigned to one of the larger rooms and climbed to the top seat of the bleacher. Through the steam, we saw Leo Tague on the opposite bench. I worked up the courage to ask, "Leo, whatever happened to the cast that adorned the corner of your bar?"

Leo blurted a few cuss words and said he didn't mind losing the cast, but it was pretty cheap for someone to steal all the raffle money that had been collected in it. It was all we could do to suppress our surprise and not reveal we'd had something to do with its disappearance.

INTERLUDE: THE MYSTERY OF CAMP RUIN

On the last weekend of the season, the snow was still too deep for us to search around Camp Ruin for the cast. When we returned the next fall, we combed the area, but we never found a trace of it or its contents.

Camp Ruin was razed in 1975. The sauna that the group visited was the former Camp Bruin, which Brud Folger had moved half a mile east in the late 1960s. It's now Hugs Restaurant. Leo Tague moved "The Infirmary" and incorporated it into Chateau des Tagues, which stood where the SugarBowl is today.

6

Invasion of the Ski Bums

ONE DAY IN THE MID-1940S, A STOREKEEPER, A DRUGSTORE OWNER, and a passel of schoolboys piled into an old Dodge panel truck and set out from Kingfield to look for ski terrain on Bigelow Mountain, a long, multi-summited ridge in the Longfellow range. Chances are they didn't see another vehicle as they made their way north through the

Austrian Werner Rothbacher (far left) was hired as a Sugarloaf ski instructor in 1957. He became the ski school director the following year and spent ten years teaching the Wedeln technique, a maneuver developed in Austria. With him are, from left to right, Andy Schoenthaner, Tom Reynolds, unidentified, Bob Scott, Leo Tague, Tom MacDonald, and Leslie Nichols. COURTESY OF SUGARLOAF SKI CLUB

Carrabassett River Valley. In those days, it was common for an hour or more to pass between cars traveling the stretch of Route 27 between Kingfield and Stratton. With a combined population of seventy-eight, Jerusalem and Crockertown had little to draw anyone who wasn't hunting, fishing, or working for Dead River Company or Great Northern Paper, which owned nearly all the land.[22]

The explorers almost certainly saw horses, however. When they turned off Route 27 at the shuttered Lawrence Plywood mill, they followed dirt County Crosscut Road (a.k.a. Cross Road, and now, Carriage Road) past a red barn and pasture where Dead River and its contractors kept a few dozen draft horses. In the mid-twentieth century, horses were still the principal means of dragging logs out of Maine forests, a mostly wintertime task. The teams that worked in the valley brought the wood to clearings on logging roads like County Crosscut, where it was stockpiled until trucks picked it up and carried it to mills in Madison, Farmington, and Stratton.

No lumber was being sawn in the valley anymore. The retired plywood plant was the only mill still standing. Dead River used it for storage, and its land supervisor, Ken Packard, garaged his 1931 Model A roadster there.[23] When he wasn't managing the independent "jobbers" who logged and hauled trees on Dead River's timberlands, Packard cruised the forest looking for the next year's cut.

Hugh Gilmore, meanwhile, came up from Kingfield to tend the horses and graze them in the pasture adjacent to the barn. An electric fence enclosed the expanse of golden grass, one side running along the Carrabassett's east bank, which allowed the horses to wade into the river to drink. "My dad would let me go up to Huston Brook Road and unhook

---

22. Great Northern Paper bought most of Crockertown in 1905, and Dead River bought most of Jerusalem in 1908.

23. The mill was still standing, but barely, as the winter of 1958 unfolded. Then the snow came—and came and came. "The building had a one-pitch roof, and it had to have 6 to 7 feet of snow on it," Bill Gilmore said. "One night, it was raining, and Ken Packard said to my dad, 'If you want that car, go get it tonight.' I'll never forget coming up here with my older brother and dad and opening up that door. We went in and hooked a chain on that Model A roadster and pulled it out and left it in that yard for the night. The next morning, the mill was flat."

Employees of the newly formed Sugarloaf Mountain Corporation on the mountain in 1955. From left: F. Donald Brooks, Mickey Durrell, Amos Winter, Hollie Sturgis, and Dick French. COURTESY OF SUGARLOAF SKI CLUB

the gate and holler to those horses," recalled Gilmore's son Bill, who, as a preschooler in the early 1950s, sometimes accompanied his father. "They'd come charging across the river. I'd get out of the way, and down the track they'd go. They didn't need any guidance. They knew where they were going."

When the panel truck passed by the barn on its way to Bigelow Mountain, it was laying down a different sort of track, though no one, not even the truck's occupants, knew it at the time. Imagine the dust the truck's wheels spun into the air, settling onto the valley and granting it a theretofore inconceivable future, one in which A-frames would sprout along Cross County Road, airplanes would land in the pasture, and a career serving a yet-to-be-created town awaited a grownup Bill Gilmore. And in that barn, a young, ragtag group of college students, Maine Brahmins, tradespeople, suit-and-tie executives, and assorted misfits would drink and pull pranks, drink and dance, and drink and plot a (very civil) rebellion.

Amos in the snowfields in 1962. COURTESY OF SUGARLOAF SKI CLUB

Amos and Alice Winter at the lift-ticket desk in 1956. COURTESY OF SUGARLOAF SKI CLUB

STOUTHEARTED SKIERS
AND INTREPID INVESTORS

The general-store owner who organized that trip to Bigelow Mountain was, of course, Amos Winter, the future father of Sugarloaf ski resort. For years, Winter had been a springtime regular at Tuckerman Ravine, the steep, undeveloped cirque on Mount Washington's southeast face that's legendary among daredevil skiers. As he entered his mid-forties, however, Winter was intent on finding a local alternative to the two-and-a-half-hour drive to Pinkham Notch in New Hampshire.

Hence the scouting trip to Bigelow, probably sometime in 1944 or spring 1945. Winter's companions that day were pharmacist Fred "Buster" Morrison and six of the Kingfield teenagers he'd taught to ski on the hill in his Kingfield backyard: Howard Dunham, Mickey Durrell, Dick French, Howard McClure, Robert "Stub" Taylor, and Odlin Thompson. "On [Bigelow's] broad northerly flank, the potential for a ski trail of nearly 3,000 vertical feet was revealed to Amos as he explored the terrain with Fred Morrison," the late John Christie, Sugarloaf's general manager from 1965 to 1968, writes in *The Story of Sugarloaf*. Liking what they

A 1962 newspaper ad for Chateau des Tagues. COURTESY OF CHATEAU DES TAGUES

saw, the men and their proteges returned many times over that summer to carve a ski trail that followed the Appalachian Trail (AT) from Avery Peak to just below a rocky promontory named Old Man's Head. From there, the route descended north along a Civilian Conservation Corps trail. "Starting in the winter of 1945–46," Christie continues, "the Bigelow Boys, as they came to be known, enjoyed the deep snows and challenging terrain some 20 miles from Kingfield."

Their fledgling ski area lasted but two seasons. In 1948, Central Maine Power began cutting trees and burning brush around the base of Bigelow as it prepared to build a dam at Long Falls on the Dead River and create the twenty-six-mile-long hydroelectric reservoir that would flood Flagstaff village—and the Bigelow Boys' access to their trail. Undeterred, Winter turned his sights on Sugarloaf Mountain. He, his brother Erland, and the Bigelow Boys skied its snowfields that winter. On Easter weekend, they were accompanied by four Bowdoin and Colby college students who'd gotten wind of their project. "We carried our skis and climbed in our ski boots," one of the students, Phineas Sprague, wrote in a remembrance for the Sugarloaf Ski Club. "The wind had blown most of the snow off the trail, and after a while we were on top, trying to keep our skis from blowing out of our hands. Stepping off the wind-cleared summit, we were up to our waists in powder snow. With skis on shoulders, it was a good task to find the trail through the thick undergrowth and around the trees. Erland sped down with giant steps on his snowshoes, and as for Amos, after a while he put on his skis with skins (strips of sealskin attached to the bottom of the skis). He did pretty well, but he couldn't keep up with Erland. Very clearly, we had found what we were seeking: good terrain with lots of snow. We told the Winters that we'd be back as we departed for Brunswick."

It just so happened that while the Bigelow Boys were exploring Sugarloaf, the Maine Development Commission in Augusta was actively coveting New Hampshire's robust ski economy. The commission summoned representatives of clubs managing community ski hills around the state and formed the Maine Ski Council, whose mission was to find Pine Tree State counterparts to Cranmore, Wildcat, and Cannon. In 1949, after Winter gave council members a tour, Sugarloaf—Maine's second

A-plus fames: The camps in Carrabassett's A-frame village have been altered every which way since they were built in the 1960s. AUTHOR

Coach Jim Fitzpatrick with Sugarloaf Ski Club junior program racers Danny Baxter, Gail Blackburn, and Tim Skaling in the late 1960s. This program was the seed for Carrabassett Valley Academy. COURTESY OF SUGARLOAF SKI CLUB

highest mountain at 4,237 feet—rose to the top of a list that included Bigelow (4,145 feet), Mount Blue (3,192 feet), and Saddleback (4,121), all in Franklin County, as well as twin-peaked Baldpate in Oxford County (3,789 feet).

"Sugarloaf is right in Maine's belt of heaviest snow," Maine Development Commission executive director Everett F. Greaton explained to the *Portland Press Herald* in December. "It comes early and stays late, and the exposure is right to prevent early melting." The biggest challenge was not Sugarloaf's remoteness, he added; rather, it was finding the money required to carve trails and build lifts, lodges, and other infrastructure. "Sun Valley in Idaho and Aspen in Colorado, both far from any center of population, have proven that accessibility is not so much of a factor," Greaton said. "If funds could be found to develop the slope, to put in a

Robert Anderson (a.k.a. Pea Shot) was one of the early Sugarloaf Ski Club's junior program racers who rose to the national ladder.
COURTESY OF SUGARLOAF SKI CLUB

modern chair lift, and establish a hotel or camps, Sugarloaf would be one of the greatest winter sports areas in New England."

Supporters organized the Sugarloaf Mountain Ski Club and, with mountain owner Great Northern Paper's blessing, the Merrow family's gift of a right of way over their land near Bigelow Station, and Dead River Company's bulldozer, they began building an access road and cutting a

This postcard shows the Sugarloaf Inn in the 1960s, when it was built and operated by Don and Maryann Pfeifle. COURTESY OF DONALD KENNETH SIEBURG/SIEBURG POSTCARD COMPANY

trail designed by Franconia, New Hampshire, ski-area architect Sel Hannah. Among the volunteers that summer of 1950 was Kingfield teenager and future Sugarloaf ski instructor Harvey Packard. Years later, in an interview with *SKI* magazine's Krista Crabtree, he described a DIY construction zone, where people mud-packed dynamite onto boulders, lit the fuse, and "ran like hell." Amos Winter, he added, was a genial motivator, cajoling everyone to toil on. For that, and for his vision, the trail was named Winter's Way.

Winter's Way attracted adventurers as soon as there was enough snow to ski, and the *Bangor Daily News* included the trail in its weekly ski column for the first time on January 5, 1951: "A mile-long trail, bushed out to a 50-foot width, has been completed. From all reports, the intrepid skier who climbs this 2,000-foot drop will find snowfields of unexcelled alpine skiing."

Intrepid indeed. The two-mile Access Road was exceedingly rough and prone to washouts during thaws, and the steep hike to the snowfields took more than two hours. Ski-shop owner Harvey Boynton summed up a day of skiing for *SKI*: "One trail, one climb, one run."

Doc and Joni Blanchard in front of their A-frame, probably in the early 1970s.

For the first few years, Sugarloaf was primarily a locals' playground and a once-a-winter romp for everyone else. Yet the area grew steadily, nurtured by club members who spent their summer weekends cutting trees and picking rocks off the trails and by businesspeople who donated tools, equipment, and materials. Each year brought something new. In 1952, it was the first Sugarloaf Schuss competition, which attracted forty-seven racers who climbed to the snowfields accompanied by volunteers setting out poles and flags. In 1953, the club opened a warming hut and installed the first lift, a seven-hundred-foot-long rope tow on the lowest section of Winter's Way. In 1954, Great Northern Paper gave the club a twenty-year lease for the use of Sugarloaf. The rent was $25 per year.

The game changer arrived in mid-March 1955, when several members of the ski club formed the publicly held Sugarloaf Mountain Corporation

Motel owner "Ma" Judson chats with (from left) Red Stallion owner Ed Rogers, Sugarloaf general manager Harry Baxter, and Chateau des Tagues owner Leo Tague, probably in the mid-1960s. COURTESY OF SUGARLOAF SKI CLUB

(SMC). They were a well-connected bunch that included Robert "Bunny" Bass of the Wilton-based shoe manufacturer G. H. Bass; Farmington insurance agent (and son of the F&M railroad's doctor, Charles Bell) Richard Bell; state senator Ben Butler, of Farmington; Bath Iron Works hull engineer George Cary II; H. King Cummings, president of Guilford Industries textiles mills; Waterville dentist William Kierstead; Farmington fuel dealer C. Richard Luce; Augusta stockbroker George Mendall; Hallowell state representative Bill Vaughan; and several other Pine Tree State power brokers. Amos Winter was named general manager. Within a month, the corporation's $100,000 stock offering, issued at $10 per share, was more than one-quarter subscribed—and the prospectus hadn't even been delivered yet. The Sugarloaf Ski Club received one thousand shares in exchange for its facilities and the Access Road. The club would continue to organize races and other events on the mountain.

Development of a large, modern ski area was assured, SMC president Bass announced at the end of April. "Present and immediate development is part of a master plan for the Sugarloaf area, and possibly a million dollars and more eventually being invested in new inns, bunkhouses for college skiers, an additional T-bar lift extending to the top of the mountain, and larger scale development of the left-handed side of the slope, as well as one long or two shorter chairlifts on this side." In fact, Bass added, SMC was just a few weeks away from breaking ground on a 3,757-foot T-bar and two new trails.

DESTINATION: SUGARLOAF

All of a sudden, Sugarloaf was no longer just a locals' mountain. When the T-bar made its debut in the winter of 1955–1956, skiers with SMC connections set about buying or building getaways in Crockertown: Brothers Jonathan, Roger, and Norton Luce were among the first, buying a fur-trapper's cabin in the former Bigelow Station freight yard. Richard Bell bought a parcel of land there as well and then convinced his mother, Annie, to buy the station building, which the family used as a camp. One mile south, SMC directors Bill Kierstead, George Mendall, and King Cummings leased quarter-acre lots from Scott Paper, which had purchased most of Great Northern Paper's lands in the Carrabassett

Grand Opening
IN SKI LAND

SUGARLOAF MOTEL

YOUR HOME AWAY FROM HOME
- KNOTTY PINE DINING ROOM with FIREPLACE
- COCKTAIL LOUNGE
- FAMILY ACCOMMODATIONS ● SKI DORMS

AMERICAN and EUROPEAN PLAN
DANCING – TV – EXCELLENT HUNTING & FISHING
RATES: $7.50 to $9.50   This Includes
                            Breakfast & Dinner

IRV AND EDNA JUDSON
PLAN to VISIT US THIS WEEKEND

CARRABASSET,   MAINE

A newspaper ad for Jerusalem Township's newest motel.

River Valley. They built their camps on a curve that, in 1957, would be separated from Route 27 in a highway-straightening project and renamed Campbell Field Road. Likewise, Bunny Bass and George Cary built their huts on a section of highway that became Woodcock Road.[24]

In 1958, Irv and Edna Judson built the valley's first new hostelry since the turn of the century. Judson's Sugarloaf Motel typified the utilitarian motel architecture of the time: It was a single, long, one-story building with fourteen rooms, a restaurant arranged around a center hallway, and, in the basement (to satisfy liquor license requirements in northern Maine at that time), a bar in which the only entertainment was a jukebox. Judson's was the sum total of the Sugarloaf après-ski scene for the next three years.

In 1959, on the heels of Bunny Bass's optimistic forecast, Leo Tague, a member of a Coplin lumbering family, bought the Record family's

Postcard for Judson's Sugarloaf Motel in the early 1970s. On the back it reads, "Pleasant Rooms and Hospitality. The Home of Good Food. Hunting, Fishing and Skiing. Open Year Round." COURTESY OF JAY AND WENDY WYMAN

---

24. Scott Paper purchased most of the Crockertown land that had belonged to Great Northern in 1955. Scott leased the quarter-acre lots for $25 a year in 1956. By the early 1980s, the rent had risen to $200 a year.

properties in Jerusalem, including Record's Camps and, on the opposite side of Route 27, their store/restaurant and three century-old houses. When a fire destroyed the store two years later, Tague wasted no time fretting. He immediately hired contractor Emery Hall to build a bigger place across the street. Hall worked so fast that Leo and his first wife, Jean, opened Chateau des Tagues to hunters that fall. Their target market, however, was the ski crowd. The Tagues emphasized their proximity to the slopes in advertisements for "Sugarloaf's finest accommodations," "the steakhouse of the valley," and "Sugarloaf's only chateau." Chalet-style flourishes decorated the exterior of the main building that housed the restaurant and bar. Two wings contained five motel rooms each. Tague twice expanded his Chateau, first with a rear addition containing a bunkroom, guest room, and an apartment for him and his wife, and later by relocating three of the six hunting camps that composed White's Cabins on Bigelow Hill.[25]

As a member of the Sugarloaf Ski Club who'd helped cut trails alongside Amos Winter, Tague knew that skiers wanted more than a meal and a bed after a day on the slopes; they wanted to have fun. Chateau des Tagues offered live music in a bar tended by young men who slung drinks mainly to support their skiing habit. A guitarist and drummer, Tague often played with the band. Carrabassett Valley contractors and philanthropists Clem and Rolande Begin found their first jobs in the valley working for Tague as chef and head of housekeeping, respectively. They remembered their former boss as a warm and gregarious host. "Everybody was friends with Leo," Rolande said. "He was good to us."

Tague, who died in 2001, was an influential member of the community. He was a member of the first ski patrol, a ski instructor, and president of the Sugarloaf Ski Club when it sponsored its first United States Eastern Amateur Ski Association race in 1960. He spearheaded

---

25. One of those cabins is all that remains of Chateau des Tagues today—it's the log structure with porch next to the snowmobile garage at the corner of Route 27 and Old Huse Mill Road. One of the three houses from Tague's first lodging venture also still stands. In the Chateau's heyday, it was known as the Hovel, which Tague offered to travelers when his inn was full. A night in the Hovel cost just $1 per guest—a bargain if you didn't mind that the closest bathroom was across the street in the Chateau.

the effort that persuaded Rangeley Power Company to extend its lines through the valley in 1961. A pilot, he laid out the airstrip that became Sugarloaf Regional Airport, and he was the airport's first manager. As partners in a construction business, he and Clem Begin built a number of camps and houses. After Tague sold the Chateau, it underwent a series of owners and name changes, including Macho's (which later moved across the street), Carrabassett Yacht Club, Mayor's Place, Narrow Gauge Inn, and Carrabassett Inn and Grill. In 2014, the building was razed to make way for the SugarBowl bowling alley.

THE NEW SETTLERS

In May 1958, Jean Woodbury spent her weekends skiing at Sugarloaf instead of doing what her mother was prodding her to do: plan her June wedding to G. Norton Luce. Reflecting on their conversations decades later, Jean Luce (that's right, Luce—she made it to the church on time) conceded that she'd done little to ease her mother's anxiety:

"When are we going to plan the wedding?"

"Oh, when the skiing ends!"

Luce had skied at Sugarloaf for the first time the year before and had recently taken lessons with its new ski school director, Austrian Werner Rothbacher. High on newcomer's euphoria, she couldn't resist the extended season. "It was an awesome ski year," she said. "There was so much snow that the lift shacks were buried in it, and they offered a day's lift ticket to anyone who would help shovel them out. Norton was one of them."

Norton, who died in 2009, had been an active member of the Sugarloaf Ski Club since its founding. After Jean married him, she dove into organizing the club's races, which had grown in number and complexity since the first Sugarloaf Schuss. She made frequent trips between the couple's home in Farmington and Sugarloaf, and on weekends the couple stayed at Norton and his brothers' log cabin in the old Bigelow Station rail yard. By 1964, Jean was spending more time in Crockertown than Farmington, heading home only to do laundry and shop for groceries. "At that point, I asked, 'Why are we still "living" in Farmington?'"

And so the Luces, now in their mid-twenties and parents of two toddlers, became year-rounders on the mountain.[26] The Luces' children, Johanna and Bob, brought the under-fifteen population living between Kingfield and Stratton to twelve—the most since the first U.S. census in 1790.

"For a while, I had been the only kid," said Cindy Tague, who was eight when her father and mother got into the lodging business. "I rode to school with Freddy the mailman. Freddy made two trips a day from Farmington to Coburn Gore. He'd stop in the morning and pick me up and take me to school in Stratton. On his way back, he'd drive me home."

In 1961, the state hired a driver to take ten-year-old Cindy to school in Kingfield with twins Hank and Luke Pfeifle (also ten) and John Pfeifle (twelve).[27] The boys lived at the new Sugarloaf Inn, which their parents, Don and Maryann Pfeifle, had built within walking distance of the ski trails (the oldest Pfeifle child, Peter, was away at prep school). The Pfeifles hailed from Bellport on Long Island's south shore, but they were well acquainted with western Maine through summers spent on Clearwater Lake in Industry. Lake friends had pointed Don to Sugarloaf when he told them he was looking to get out of the children's clothing manufacturing business.

"Sugarloaf was still just getting started, really," Hank Pfeifle said. "You had Tagues and you had Judson's, but nothing in the way of accommodations on the mountain. The [SMC] basically said, hey, if you build an inn, we'll give you a 100-year lease on the property."

While the inn was being constructed in the summer of 1960, Don took courses at Cornell University's hotel school. He and Maryann opened for business a few months later during Christmas school vacation week.[28] Despite having no friends living nearby, the Pfeifle boys never

---

26. After the Luces moved to Sugarloaf Village, Norton founded Mountain Fuel Co. and Valley Gas Co. at the urging of his grandfather, George Luce, the founder of Farmington Oil Company and Luce Oil Company. Bob Luce later assumed ownership of Valley Gas and Oil, which he sold in 2022.

27. By 1967, there were enough school-age children living in the valley for the state to provide a nine-passenger bus to take them to Kingfield. The bus was owned and operated by the state. Jack Hargreaves of New Portland was the driver.

28. It may have been the Pfeifles' enterprise that inspired the Anson-based Somerset Telephone Co. to create the Bigelow exchange (237) in 1961. In addition to Sugarloaf Inn, the exchange had six other accounts: Sugarloaf base lodge, Chateau des Tagues, Judson's Motel, Norton Luce, Donald Pfeifle, and hunting-camp-owner-turned-year-rounder Harold Anderson.

felt deprived of companions in an inn that accommodated 103 guests. "At Christmas, we saw the same set of friends year after year," Luke said. "Another set of friends would come in for February school vacation. Same thing in April. You couldn't beat it, really."

"It gave us exposure to all types of people," Hank added. "We had jobs—we did dishes and stuff in the kitchen, and that's where we met the ski bums. They were college kids, and they were fun. They worked for my parents in exchange for a season ticket, tips, and a place to stay in our dorm."

Meanwhile, the population of camp owners continued to grow. Like Scott Paper, Dead River leased small lots to individuals who built cabins on them. Beginning in 1959, Waterville business partners Dave Rollins and Wes Sanborn built several A-frames around Carriage and Huston Brook roads. One of the first to buy was *Bangor Daily News* reporter and unofficial Sugarloaf cheerleader Bud Leavitt, who convinced several others to join him in the fledgling village. Other camps were do-it-yourself affairs, like the one on Campbell Field Road belonging to Liz and Herbert Hoeffler. The Hoefflers met at the Sugarloft dormitory in Kingfield in March 1959 and became engaged that June. With the help of friends, they finished building their camp in time for their December honeymoon there. "We had been lugging building materials up from Massachusetts every weekend," Liz recalled. The next summer, they and their friends went down to the river and to old mill sites to collect rocks and bricks for the fireplace. "We dumped them in a huge pile out in front of the cabin and sorted them on our hands and knees. We scraped the old mortar off the bricks."

With so few restaurants and bars, the camp owners—most of them in their twenties and early thirties—took turns hosting après-ski, which consisted of potluck suppers, plenty of beer and wine, and dancing to a record spinning on a turntable. The valley version of bar hopping was going from camp to camp.

"Everyone knew everyone else," Hoeffler said. "You knew the lift attendant. You knew the guy who ran the ski school. You'd go to Tagues' and all the people drinking and dancing were your friends."

The hotels, eateries, and other businesses that did pop up have entered into Carrabassett Valley folklore as pioneers in the heady but financially risky period that preceded the town's founding. A few were off-center, wayward ventures that couldn't have taken root anywhere but an unorganized place with few rules and little polish. Near Bigelow Station were Charles and Elinor Clark's twenty-one-room Capricorn Lodge (whose kitschy Swiss chalet–style flourishes were initially trumpeted as "Barbarian décor" in a local business association brochure) and Dick and Mary Fountain's Lumberjack Lodge (which took so long to build that its motto—"Ready for you in '62"—had to be updated to "Ready for more in '64"). "If I'd known what I was getting myself into, I would have joined the Foreign Legion," Dick Fountain joked years later.[29]

In Carrabassett, Rollins and Sanborn bought Dead River's vacant barn, its former tenants having been supplanted by skidders and logging machinery, and converted it into the Red Stallion Inn. Some people reported seeing decades' worth of manure being carted away, but on rainy days, regulars who shimmied on the spongy dance floor noted a distinct odor that convinced them some had been left behind. Billy Jones and Brud Folger built the wood-heated Sugarloaf Sauna at the corner of Route 27 and Town Line Road and hired their friend and fellow musician "Uncle Al" Scheeren to run it in exchange for free saunas and lodging in a tiny house on the property.[30] Across Town Line Road from the sauna, in a prefabricated log cabin, was David Brophy's Mogul Delicatessen, prized for its Italian sandwiches and a Saturday special of baked beans and brown bread. 'Til Midnight, a small grocery, operated seven days a week in one of the Tague-owned houses next to the Hovel.[31]

'Til Midnight's owner, Francis "Andy" Andrews, was a retired newspaperman on a quest to learn "what made Maine tick." He'd already worked on a chicken farm and in a Biddeford textile mill. For three weeks before 'Til Midnight's grand opening, Andrews and his wife, Beverly, spent their days scrubbing decades of oil-stove soot from the walls and refinishing the tar paper–covered floors. At night they enjoyed candlelit dinners at

29. The Capricorn now serves as faculty housing for Carrabassett Valley Academy. The Lumberjack is Lumberjack Condominiums with eight one-bedroom units.

30. The sauna building now houses Hugs Italian restaurant.

31. After 'Til Midnight closed, the building was a seafood restaurant and then a Mexican restaurant. It was later destroyed by fire. The building that housed the Hovel was still standing as of 2022.

Chateau des Tagues. The day before they opened, they stood outside in the swirling snow and admired their work. "We were elated," Andrews wrote in a feature published by the *Boston Herald*. "Wolf, moose, and bear gloves hung from the window, with mukluks, snowshoes, and knapsack. The lighted case displayed imported cheeses, beer, meat, vegetables, and milk. Shelves held staples and party foods. The pizza oven was ready to give forth robust spicy Italian aroma to blend with the wondrously clean, crisp air."

The only store open until midnight within sixty miles of Sugarloaf, 'Til Midnight attracted a diverse and eccentric clientele. "Our customers have included a bush pilot-to-be, sailor, one-legged hunter, and a doctor in whites with a stethoscope about his neck," Andrews wrote. "You've got the picture when you add a hearse adorned with the words 'We Deliver,' filled with skiers and their equipment in what was also their sleeping quarters. The Sugarloaf-Carrabassett Valley way of life sets a pattern in a troubled world. There is tolerance. It is an untroubled life with simplicity. Even without restrictions, the region sets an admirable example of harmony between The Establishment and Youth Movement, who utilize half a dozen lodges, more than 600 chalets, eight ski lifts, and 35 miles of ski trails." The article included a photograph of a small plane at the 'Til Midnight gas pump—a re-creation, perhaps, of the day Ted Jones, one of the valley's early skier pilots, ran out of fuel mid-air, landed on Route 27, and coasted to the store.

Pilots kept their planes at Leo Tague's airstrip behind the Chateau. Jones, Sugarloaf's comptroller, was known for such feats as splashing down in the Red Stallion's swimming pool. "Harvey Boynton and Leo Tague fly by instruments; Dutch Demshar by night; Ted Jones, by the grace of God," Leola Defoe wrote in the *Irregular*. "It's not that people are afraid for Ted's safety, but every time he takes off, they send Meg Hutchinson down to the Sugarloaf Chapel to light a candle. Ted carries so many good luck charms in his plane that it has a 300-pound weight load before he even gets in. However, it's a sturdy ship—as well it should be since Ted had to send in an astonishing total of 167 box tops to get it. Ted's reputation for air acrobatics (which are even more impressive when you consider they are all unplanned) has become well known and, as a consequence, a sign has recently been erected at Tague's airstrip: 'Warning: Jones is up; nobody else can use the sky.'"

A CONSTRUCTION BLIZZARD

The newcomers who built dwellings and businesses in a pair of railroad ghost towns found some reassurance about the soundness of their investments on the mountain, where Sugarloaf Mountain Corporation was aggressively pursuing its vision of a big, modern ski resort. In the fifteen years that followed Bunny Bass's announcement, SMC had built and expanded a new base lodge, enlarged the parking lot, cut new trails with names borrowed from logging lingo, and installed more lifts. John Christie, who had worked his way up from ski patroller to Amos Winter's assistant manager, took over for the retiring Winter in 1965 and assumed oversight of the construction of "the mighty gondola," a top-to-bottom lift with 50 four-passenger cars. Traversing 8,430 feet of terrain and rising 2,350 feet, it was the longest such conveyance in the East, capable of transporting skiers to the summit in fourteen minutes. That, along with the rebranding of the resort as Sugarloaf/USA, were the boldest expressions of SMC's ambitions to date. The state supported the marketing effort by changing the name of Crockertown to Sugarloaf Township, population twenty, in 1963.[32]

Competitions like the U.S. Junior National Championships in 1959 and NCAA Ski Championships in 1967 got the attention of national newspapers and magazines. So did Sugarloaf's first international (in name only) event in 1968: the World Heavyweight Championships for amateur skiers weighing over two hundred pounds. The event was one of many championed by Red Stallion owner Ed Rogers, *Irregular* editor Dave Rolfe, and Sugarloaf general manager Harry Baxter, who were inspired by their very large drinking and skiing buddy, Edward "Lard" Dugan. Contestants were weighed on farm scales and charged an entry fee of 2 cents per pound, with proceeds donated to the Pine Tree Society (then the Pine State Crippled Children Fund). Though the World Heavyweight Championship would meet with disapproval today, the contestants were enthusiastic and the event received national attention.

---

32. Representative Harold Hutchins, of Kingfield, introduced the bill.

SMC wasn't into real-estate development yet, but some of its board members were. They had formed the Bigelow Corporation in 1960 and anted up $10,000 apiece to purchase the 1,800-acre "Merrow tract" and develop what board president George "Tim" Terry III called "a carefully planned forest playground."[33] Bigelow hired Joseph Sewall Company, then of Old Town, to draw up a development plan, which eventually became Sugarloaf Village 1 (where the Luces were the first buyers) and Sugarloaf Village 2. Bigelow swamped out Brackett Brook Road and improved it to the hill crest, where it placed a model home—a chalet prefabricated by the Massachusetts-based Stan-Mar company.[34] When the Luces purchased their two one-acre lots beyond the improved section of the road, Bigelow laid down gravel to their driveway and put another chalet on the lot next door. There resided singer and comedian Jud Strunk, hired by Bigelow to sell lots. Eight years away from national fame as a cast member on the TV series *Rowan and Martin's Laugh-In*, Strunk ferried

---

1962

Leo Tague, the Sugarloaf ski resort operator, is snapping his suspenders—the ones holding his hunting trousers and not the stretch slacks. He whacked down a 9-point, 174-pound buck in the Kingfield country, and you couldn't hold him today with a team of wild horses. —*Bangor Daily News*, November 30

---

33. Besides Terry, Bigelow's board members were Harvey Boynton, vice president; Adrian Asherman, secretary/treasurer; Ralph M. Clark, clerk; and Alden Macdonald, Wadsworth Hinds, William Kierstead, Dr. Edwin Ervin, Parker Poole, and Emil "Jay" Winter. Once part of Prouty & Miller's holdings, the Merrow tract stretched from Caribou Pond to Town Line Road. The Prouty and Miller families sold the land to Mark H. Merrow and Leon Wardwell in 1920; Wardwell sold his share to Merrow in 1938; Merrow willed it to his daughters, Evelyn and Mary, that same year; and Evelyn sold her interest to Mary. Prior to selling to the Bigelow Corporation in 1960, Mary White had conveyed one parcel to the Capricorn Lodge and one to developers of camps in the Bigelow Station area. White was the owner with her second husband of White's Cabins—the same cabins that Leo Tague had moved and cobbled together for his motel.

34. The model chalet was later sold to Robert Porteous of Portland, a philanthropist, state senator, and owner of the venerable Maine department store chain, Porteous, Mitchell and Braun.

potential buyers around on a then-novel red Polaris snowmobile. He, his wife, Marti, and their son, Rory, were the Luces' neighbors for about two years before moving to Farmington.

Sugarloaf Village was part of a larger effort to transform Jerusalem and Crockertown into a resort community. Bigelow Corporation, Dead River Company, Scott Paper, and SMC had formed the Carrabassett Valley Association to coordinate the development of the townships "in a manner consistent with the best interest of all the companies" and "in a way that will maintain the character and dignity of the whole area."

Primarily a producer of pulpwood, lumber, and veneer, Dead River saw camps and houses sprouting up like weeds on its leased lots at Spring Farm Road (another former Route 27 curve) and Poplar Stream.[35] Now it wanted to take more active role in recreational development—and not just because it was potentially lucrative. Curtis Hutchins, the company's chairman, believed opening commercial forestland to recreation protected the forest industry against "emotional and political" attacks on logging.[36] "The vacation seekers outnumber us a multiplicity to one, and they will vote that way too," he told foresters at a September 1961 gathering in Washington, D.C. Indeed, he pointed out, "the growing intensity of the conflicts" between recreational and industrial interests was the impetus for the conference, which explored how woodlands can simultaneously meet the nation's growing timber and paper needs and serve as a "refuge from mechanized life and mass neurosis."

The next month, Dead River hosted two hundred state officials, industry leaders, outdoorsmen, and reporters at the opening of Carrabassett Village, an expansion of the A-frame hamlet started by Dave Rollins and Wes Sanborn. The guests were treated to a lumberman's repast of

---

35. When Dead River offered its leased lots to the lessees for purchase in the late 1960s, a title search revealed that twenty-five of the parcels actually belonged to the state. They were part of the land, called public lots, that had been reserved for future settlement under the charter for William Bingham's Kennebec Purchase in 1753. The state took over the camp leases. In 1969, the 104th Legislature resolved to sell the twenty-five leased lots to the current lessees.

36. Hutchins, who died in 1985, had a great deal of influence in Maine and beyond. He was a Maine state representative, Bangor city councilor, and member of the United States Chamber of Commerce. He was chairman of the Aroostook and Bangor Railroad, president of St. Croix Paper Company, and a director of Scott Paper Company, State St. Bank & Trust Company, Boston, Guilford Industries in Guilford, Bangor Punta Corporation, and Merrill Trust Company in Bangor.

1968

Governor Kenneth M. Curtis and the Executive Council plan to hold a "summit conference" next Wednesday atop 4,237-foot-high Sugarloaf Mountain. The officials will ride up the mountain on gondolas, and those not wishing to ski will return by the gondola. —*Bangor Daily News*, February 28

grilled hot dogs, brown bread, and bean-hole beans. They toured model A-frames and chalets and learned about Dead River's plans to build 150 such dwellings on 100-by-100-foot lots and offer them to renters on ten-year leases at a cost of $25 a year.

Dead River soon created a recreation and land use division, headed by Curtis Hutchins's son, Christopher. This real-estate arm supplied building materials to contractors, sold firewood and propane, and offered services like house cleaning, interior design, maintenance, and snow removal. Within a few years, young Hutchins had made Dead River the Sugarloaf region's largest private recreation developer. In February 1968, the company gave a press tour of three completed houses in Redington North, its four-season luxury-home development on a ridge facing Sugarloaf. On hand was the architect, Ed Diehl, who called it "the most exciting" project of his twenty-year career: "I do not look upon this development as a second-home project. It is, in my mind, a first-home project with second-home uses." Ads for the Redington homes beckoned potential buyers with a promise that would become the motto of the future town of Carrabassett Valley: "From here on your life will never be the same."

The next year, Dead River built Valley Crossing Shopping Center, "the newest, most original skiing center in the country—east or west!" Located at the corner of Route 27 and the Carriage Road, the building was a Jenga puzzle of differently shaped boxes with vertical wood siding and steeply pitched roofs (today, it's the core of Sugarloaf resort's Village West, having been taken apart and moved up mountain in 1977). Inside were fifteen businesses, including Ayotte's general store, competitive skier Peter Webber's third ski shop (the others were in Waterville and his hometown of Farmington), and the Bag (a.k.a. Bag and Kettle), a bar and restaurant run by Webber's brother Norton (a.k.a. "Icky") and Billy Jones. That August, the shopping center and Dead River's model vacation homes were the highlight of the Maine Forest Council's eleventh annual field day. The council was keen on demonstrating that wood harvesting operations that give "due regard to forest reproduction, construction of access roads, and feeding opportunities for wildlife" can enhance recreation growth.

Faced with high costs and low profits, Dead River sold off its construction, design, services, and building materials operations in 1971, but it continued to build, adding a twenty-eight-unit condominium to its Valley Crossing property. At this point, the company had built more than two hundred A-frames and chalets at Poplar Stream and Spring Farm and more than fifty luxurious homes in Redington North and East.

In his 1972 history of Dead River, Curtis Hutchins said his father wouldn't recognize the township that his company had purchased in 1908.

1969

Fifteen years ago, the big excitement around here was the size of the bobcat population. "That's all it was, good 'cat country. Then it all changed, and now you have to look mighty hard to find a 'cat hunter." Erland Winter ought to know about such things. He was the game warden in this country. He was a bobcat hunter. "I never believed, really, that skiers would drive out the 'cat hunters. But they did, somehow." They did, alright, drove the bobcats and the hunters out of the country. Now the whole world of skiing knows about Maine's highest ski hill. . . . The same ground where Warden Winter tramped is populated by fine hotels serving excellent food and providing all the services of a city-operated complex. —*Bangor Daily News*, January 30

"There is ample evidence in the early pages of this Dead River story that my father was a far-sighted man," he wrote. "However, even if he possessed a crystal ball, it is hard to believe that he could have foreseen the day when Jerusalem Township would be swarming with human beings bent on breaking their legs by sliding down Sugarloaf Mountain. As a matter of fact ... I have to go over to Carrabassett every once and a while myself and see it to believe it." Sugarloaf, he continued, "dragged us out of the relative peace and quiet of the land business into the hurly-burly of the real estate business."

The real-estate business had also indirectly dragged Dead River into the town-creation business. In the late 1960s, the state of Maine was working on revising regulations for its unorganized territories, including zoning to regulate growth and a process for assessing taxes. The newly created Land Use Regulatory Commission (now the Land Use Planning Commission) was identifying environmental assets and introducing restrictions to protect them. That plan troubled one of its members—Chris Hutchins. Hutchins wanted Dead River's lands out from under LURC jurisdiction, and he believed the valley's small but growing population might share his concerns, particularly with their fifteen-mill taxation rate.

He was right. On March 15, 1971, the citizens of Jerusalem, Sugarloaf, and Wyman gathered in the Sugarloaf base lodge to hear Hutchins and likeminded residents make their case and learn about a bill being presented to the state legislature that would permit the three townships to form one town named Carrabassett Valley. The meeting selected insurance and real-estate professional Preston Jordan to represent them in Augusta and elected a committee to study the pros and cons.[37]

Hutchins had planted the seed. Now a bunch of ski bums were going to make it grow.

---

37. The committee was made up of one resident from each township (Preston Jordan of Jerusalem, Jean Luce of Sugarloaf, and Maurice Skaling of Wyman), one executive from each large landowner (Bob Firtney of Huber Corporation, Harvey Boynton of Bigelow Corporation, and Chris Hutchins of Dead River Company), and one nonresident land and chalet owner (John Conti of Bangor).

Interlude

A GRAND OPENING IN SKI LAND

Edna Judson was skeptical when her husband, Irv, drove her to tiny Jerusalem Township in 1956 in an attempt to persuade her to relocate their Unity hotel business. Edna had never heard of Jerusalem or the Sugarloaf ski area that Irv believed would send them so much business they'd never have to work again. He was right, but only about the amount of business. When Judson's Motel celebrated its twenty-fifth anniversary in 1983, Edna, then seventy-eight and widowed, was still welcoming guests. "I've never worked harder," she told the *Original Irregular*.

The first new hostelry and restaurant of the ski era, Judson's Sugarloaf Motel introduced nightlife to the Carrabassett River Valley and was the place where Jerusalem residents voted in October 1971 on whether to incorporate as the town of Carrabassett Valley. The Judsons dropped "Sugarloaf" from their business's name not long after the Sugarloaf Inn opened in late 1960 to avoid confusion.

The Judsons fell in love with the valley when they went scouting that day in 1956. And after they opened their fourteen-room motel in February 1957, the valley fell in love with them. The ski bums who stopped in for Edna's comfort food enjoyed listening to Irv tell about his friendship with Bing Crosby, whom he'd met when Crosby was a guest at the couple's hotel in Unity. Edna, rarely seen without an apron over her dress, cooked homestyle meals (her specialty was roast beef and potatoes) and made sure her clientele was well fed, even the young, perpetually broke ski bums who sometimes couldn't afford to pay. "She loved us all and always made us feel welcome," Carrabassett Valley resident Joni Blanchard told the *Irregular* in 2015. "No one knew her name was Edna. We all just called her Ma."

The Judsons are believed to be the first people to purchase land in Jerusalem from Dead River Company, which had owned most of the township for four decades (the people who built camps on Dead River land in the 1950s were lessees). They paid $2,000 for their four-acre parcel on Route 27 and agreed to erect a building worth at least $30,000 within a year.

"Grand Opening in Ski Land" trumpeted their half-page ad in the *Bangor Daily News* in March 1957. Rooms were $7.50–$9.50 a night, which included breakfast and dinner in the knotty-pine dining room, where there was a fireplace. Another ad promised, "Home of good food. Roast beef and homemade bread a specialty." Edna baked sixteen large loaves of bread every day, mixing and kneading the dough by hand. "That was good for me," she later reflected. "Gave me my exercise."

Though they frowned on excessive drinking, the Judsons put a cocktail lounge in the basement, a last-minute construction decision made to get a hotel liquor license, which was less costly than a license for a bar with a separate entrance. To reach the bar, customers entered the motel's center hallway and took a flight of stairs. Once there, they'd drink and dance into the wee hours. Amos Winter, who may well have loved dancing more than skiing, was among the regulars.

In the 1960s and early 1970s, Judson's bar clientele often enjoyed a joint on the back deck before making the trip downstairs, recalled Don Fowler, a member of the Carrabassett Valley History Committee. Fowler was a Sugarloaf weekender for three decades before he moved to Carrabassett Valley year-round and opened his Kingfield law office in the 1990s. "My friend used to say, one day the spaceship came down at Judson's, parked out back, the aliens went in, and they're still there."

Irv died of a heart attack at the age of sixty-one in December 1968. He was trying to save the motel furnace from water rising in the basement during a heavy rain. Edna carried on, and in the mid-1970s she hired others to cook fancier meals—or meals that sounded fancier, anyway, with French-sounding names like beef en brochette. She was eighty-one when she retired, and, in 1985, she sold the business to Lenny Brown, who hired Chuck Miller to manage it. By this time, drinks were being served upstairs in an addition named the Wee Ski Lounge. Brown sold it to Bill Pierce, who continued to operate it as Judson's, explaining when he later sold it, "We followed in Ma's footsteps and wanted to keep it that way."

After a few more ownership transfers, Adam Platz purchased and razed the building, which was in disrepair. In 2023, Platz and partners Joe Pepin and Ryan Roy built a retail plaza with several stores.

7

Coming Together

In the fall of 1968, Roger Peabody, the executive director of the United States Eastern Amateur Ski Association (USEASA), called Jean and Norton Luce, his racing circuit acquaintances from the Sugarloaf Ski Club. "We'd like to do a World Cup race at Sugarloaf in 1971," he told them.

Jean laughed. "*Here?*"

"You guys bid for the Olympics, didn't you?"

"Not exactly," she replied. That scheme had been pushed by the Boston developers of a proposed $12.5 million resort on Bigelow Mountain, and they didn't have a clue about ski competitions. The Luces, who were certified race officials, had navigated the logistics of regional and national competitions at Sugarloaf and elsewhere. They understood that an Alpine Skiing World Cup required a level of staffing, facilities, and equipment that didn't exist in western Maine.

"Well, we'd like you to do it," Peabody pressed.

Jean suggested he call Sugarloaf general manager John Christie and figured that would be the end of it.

A few hours later, the Luces' phone rang again. It was Peabody. "John Christie said yes."

What followed was a coalescing of mountain and community forces that peaked just as talk about self-government was percolating in the valley. The coordinated effort resulted in one of the best-run races of the international alpine skiing season and foreshadowed the public/private

THE RED STALLION'S BARTENDER'S TRAINING SCHOOL FEATURING CAPTAIN AMERICA ACE BARTENDER, STUDENT KARL SCHRANZ, WENDY ROGERS, AND ED ROGERS AT THE 1971 WORLD CUP RACES.

Austrian skiing legend Karl Schranz (second from left) was the first—and perhaps only—enrollee in the Red Stallion's bartending-training course, taught by Captain America (Peter Roy, far left) and Red Stallion owners Wendy Rogers and Ed Rogers. COURTESY OF SUGARLOAF SKI CLUB

partnerships that would come to guide the future town of Carrabassett Valley's approach to growth and development.

In 1968, the Alpine Skiing World Cup was in its infancy, dreamed up just two years earlier over drinks in a Chilean bar. The instigators were French sportswriter Serge Lang, French team director Honoré Bonnet, U.S. team coach Bob Beattie, and Austrian ski team lawyer Depp Sulzberger, who were together in Portillo for the 1966 World Alpine Ski Championships. Their vision was an annual competition that would borrow its name from soccer (which was the only sport with a world cup at the time) and its format from sailing (which counted finishes in select contests toward an overall ranking). According to Lang's written remembrance, the men sketched out a schedule, rules, and points system on a napkin. The next night, at the same bar, they showed it to International

Ski Federation president Marc Holder. Holder studied it for a few minutes and then asked, "What time do you want me in the press room to announce the creation of this World Cup?" The competition debuted in 1967 with a season of races at seventeen ski areas in six European and North American countries.

Just because Sugarloaf wanted the World Cup didn't mean that Sugarloaf would get it. The U.S. Ski Association, USEASA's parent organization, had to demonstrate that the mountain's course met World Cup specs for men and women's slalom and downhill races and that the area was capable of hosting one hundred or so European and North American skiers and their coaches and assistants, hundreds of race staff and volunteers, two-hundred-odd reporters, and, for each of the event's three days, thousands of spectators.

"The Sugarloaf Ski Club had a reputation for running good races," Luce said. "We had hired Werner Rothbacher from Austria to coach children. We had picked up races that had been cancelled in other places. We'd run the Junior National Championships in March 1959 and the NCAA Championships in February 1967. But we'd never tackled anything on this grand a scale."

The Luces were among a handful of club members who took jobs at the World Cup finals at Waterville Valley Resort in New Hampshire on March 21 and 22, 1969. "We were looking to see how things were done," Luce said. Waterville Valley founder Tommy Cochran gave Norton a tour of the racecourse and explained the organizer's responsibilities for on-mountain conditions, staffing, and activities related to competition. Jean got a similar course in the host's off-mountain obligations, which included everything from pre-race cocktail parties for the sponsors to housing for the athletes, coaches, and their staff. The Luces worked at the finish line alongside the public-address announcer, Norton keeping track of times and Jean organizing index cards with each racer's bib number and bio for the translator, who repeated the callouts in French and German.

An International Ski Federation official from Vancouver, Canada, came to Sugarloaf and worked with Jean, detailing everything that would be required to bring Sugarloaf's Narrow Gauge trail up to World Cup specs. The twisty-turny trail had been suitable for downhill racing when

Sugarloaf Ski Club executive director Bruce Miles holds the silver-bladed axe that was the second-place trophy in the 1971 World Cup. He found it displayed in the Ski Museum of St. Anton, Switzerland. COURTESY OF SUGARLOAF SKI CLUB

Sugarloaf Mountain Corporation trail groomers pose with state-of-the-art Thiokol snowcats that were loaned to the ski area for the World Cup.
COURTESY OF SUGARLOAF SKI CLUB

it was designed in the 1950s, but the sport had evolved. Contractors and volunteers worked three thousand hours over the next two summers, widening the trail, removing or minimizing obstacles, extending phone lines and electricity to the top of the lift, and otherwise ensuring that the course complied with rules for men's and women's international competition.

Meanwhile, Jean Luce and Christie's successor, Harry Baxter, huddled with USEASA officials to draft a twenty-plus-page bid detailing Sugarloaf's racing history, ten years' worth of snowfall and snow-depth statistics, and logistics, like how competitors from across the United States and Europe would get to a ski area that was four hours from the nearest major airport and where they'd stay once they got there.[38]

---

38. Not long after he committed Sugarloaf to the World Cup, John Christie resigned to take a position as general manager at Mt. Snow in Vermont.

In September 1969, U.S. Men's Olympic coach Willie Shaeffler and World Cup selection committee member Dr. Leland Sosman inspected Narrow Gauge and approved it as a U.S. Ski Association World Cup bid. The International Ski Federation certified Narrow Gauge in September 1970.[39]

That decision gave the Sugarloaf team four months to finalize preparations for the mid-February arrival of the world's best alpine racers—among them, American Olympian Spyder Sabich, French World Cup champ Michele Jacot, Italy's handsome young rising star Gustavo Theoni, and Austria's seemingly unbeatable two-time World Cup champ Karl Schranz.

Housing was an enormous challenge. The Sugarloaf Inn was the only on-mountain lodging, and the valley had just a handful of hostelries. Jean Luce had already spent several weeks meeting with innkeepers and camp owners from Kingfield to Stratton, asking for their help if Sugarloaf hosted the races. Now she went into high gear securing commitments. Camp owners agreed to host the hundreds of volunteer race workers. Each innkeeper pledged to house and feed one of the fourteen teams for a week—without taking a cent in compensation. "I never met any resistance. Everybody just pulled together," she said. "Once the inn owners knew what team they had, they were even more excited. They knew there would be plusses later: The mountain was going to grow. Their volume of customers was going to grow."

The Sugarloaf Area Association, a business network, hired Valley resident Carol Stratton to find accommodations for the press, a mission that reached as far as Farmington and Waterville. Sugarloaf comptroller Ted Jones sacrificed his apartment in the base lodge for use as a press room, which was outfitted with scores of typewriters, telephones, and newfangled fax machines.

Sugarloaf named its World Cup event the Tall Timber Classic. A few weeks before the races, scheduled for February 18–20, 1971, the resort agreed to simultaneously host a replacement contest for another World Cup event, the annual Alberg Kandahar ski race, which was in danger of cancellation due to a rare paucity of snow in the Alps.

---

39. As of 2022, Narrow Gauge remains the only trail in the East suitable for men's international downhill competition.

1968

Ed Rogers had a deer stolen from the Red Stallion. A nonresident hunter, who had hunted a number of seasons in Maine without success, killed his first deer in the Kingfield region. When the poor guy was at Rogers' diggings telling companions how it happened, thieves snipped the hanging rope and made off with the carcass. —*Bangor Daily News*, November 14

The racers and their entourages started arriving on February 15. Hundreds of volunteers from around New England were already in place, running errands, packing freshly fallen snow, mimeographing information packets in three languages (there were no personal computers and printers in 1971), and driving teams to and from the mountain. A Rutland, Vermont, snowmobile manufacturer sent sixteen machines and drivers to transport reporters and photographers up and down the slopes. Doctors Russell Lane of Bangor and Paul Brinkman of Farmington staffed the medical aid station for the entire time, free of charge. The Maine Forestry Department and the Maine Bureau of Civil Defense rigged up a communication system and placed staff at stations along Narrow Gauge, and the Maine National Guard provided a medical helicopter (an International Ski Federation requirement). Harry Baxter obliged the few teams that insisted on being provided with rental cars. Among them were the Italians, who saw their car as an opportunity to demonstrate their winter-driving skills. Rousted from bed at 2:00 one morning, Baxter arrived at the mountain to find them doing donuts on the Birches trail. He took away their keys.

The Swiss racers stayed at Judson's Motel, where they threw a surprise birthday party for Ma Judson during dinner one night. They presented her with a cake and Swiss souvenirs gift-wrapped in napkins, toilet paper, and tissues. The Red Stallion, which hosted the Austrian team, was more boisterous than ever as race spectators joined the regular crowd. Famous skiers like Billy Kidd and Suzy Chafee (a.k.a. "Suzy Chapstick," as she called herself in a series of lip-balm commercials) dropped in. "We had bands every night," remembered Stallion owner Ed Rogers. "It was tough for the racers to sleep." They were good sports about it, though. Karl Schranz even enrolled in "bartender training school," taught by Peter Roy (a.k.a. Captain America). "It was the best week of my life," Rogers said.

On opening day, five F106 aircraft from Loring Air Force Base's 27th Fighter Interceptor Squadron put the finishing touch on the ceremonies by flying over the mountain in missing-man formation in honor of pilots lost in the Vietnam War; at the time, public opinion against the conflict was growing.

As for the races, they went off without a hitch—almost. The one significant hiccup was a fire in the Swiss team's waxing van, which destroyed seventy pairs of skis. It started when Jim Nickerson, who ran a trash disposal business called the Groovy Garbage Company (motto: "Satisfaction or double your trash back"), lit a propane heater, unaware that the van's gas tank was full. Nickerson became an instant celebrity when an AP photo of him fighting the fire in his Groovy Garbage coveralls was carried by newspapers around the country. As for the Swiss skiers, they were able to compete thanks to other teams who loaned them skis.

Writing from the press room, *Bangor Daily News* reporter Bud Leavitt called the races a smooth-running production: "The entire Sugarloaf

---

1969

General Manager Harry Baxter of Sugarloaf Mountain and Patrick Mouligne of Paris, France, rehearsing for today's canoeski slalom at Sugarloaf, ran aground and broke up a canoe this week on the Carrabassett River. The experience taught something to Harry, since he immediately shortened the course from ten to four miles, which means canoeists in tomorrow's paddle derby will leave from Ken Packard's and finish in the area of the Carrabassett's "new bridge." Harry insists there isn't a canoeist in pants with enough ability to downstream the Carrabassett at its present water level. —*Bangor Daily News*, May 10

community, with representation from every town in Maine and from cities outside the state, is working its collective heart out to make this a winner. And as a personal aside, Mr. B. J. Bedard of Maine's Department of Economic Development has a handsomely organized press facility that includes excellent telephone service, transmitting equipment, and personnel to answer the many varied questions. He did neglect to include a supply of ear plugs. Did you ever attempt to write while a dozen guys man telephones and talk Japanese, Austrian, French, Swiss, German, and Brooklynese?"

Other than that, the Tall Timber Classic was a thoroughly Maine affair. Each morning lumberjacks scaled three flagpoles fashioned from stripped pine trees and raised the Maine, American, and International Ski Federation flags; in the evening, they'd climb back up and take the flags down. Race winners stood atop tree-stump podiums to receive their trophies—silver-plated hatchets inlaid with gold, silver, and bronze medallions, made by Snow & Nealley of Bangor. Athletes were treated to a feast of lobster and moose, the latter a last-minute donation of a road kill.

"This event contained enough drama for an entire book," John Christie writes in *The Story of Sugarloaf.* "International attention focused on Sugarloaf; copious snow and superb racing conditions; an unfortunate fire that destroyed the Swiss team's equipment; a once-in-a-lifetime chance for ski-racing fans to see the world's elite competitors in action; and an opportunity to cheer on not only the American team, but also local members thereof as well.

"The event saw the emergence of Italian slalom ace Gustavo Thoeni as the star to watch in international ski competition, as he widened his World Cup points lead following his stellar performance—including his first-ever top-ten finish in a downhill. European competitors of whom Sugarloafers had previously only read about became familiar faces: Stefano Anzi, Eddie Bruggman, Henri Duvillard, Annie Famose, Isabel Mir, Annemarie Proell, Patrick Russel, Bernhard Russi, and Karl Schranz."

Schranz, who proved to be beatable after all (he placed eleventh overall), pronounced Narrow Gauge the best-conditioned and best-prepared course of all the World Cup races so far that year. "We skiers have always known this was a good area," he said. "Now these racers will help spread the word of Sugarloaf around the world."

Might as Well Jump

The 1967 NCAA Intercollegiate Skiing Championships attracted good press for Sugarloaf, but the event has earned a place in valley lore for reasons that have nothing to do with competition—at least, not the formal kind.

Sponsored by Bates, Bowdoin, Colby, and the University of Maine, the NCAA competition was the most significant one undertaken at Sugarloaf to date, writes John Christie in *The Story of Sugarloaf*. The summer before the event, Christie, Colby ski coach Si Dunklee, and others spent "countless hours" locating and developing the required facilities, including a thirty-five-meter jump. The appropriate terrain was located up behind the Red Stallion, south of the Carriage Road between the Carrabassett River and Poplar Stream—close to the unofficial town dump.

Norwegian Bjorn Loken, skiing for the University of Utah, won the NCAA jumping championship on that earthen jump. After that, it saw occasional use for high school and college events, but mostly it just sat there, a temptation to high school students like Hanna Luce and her friends, who jumped unsupervised and unbeknownst to their parents, and to Red Stallion patrons, who jumped even though (or more likely because) they were already flying. During one of Carrabassett's infamous dump parties, Captain America (Red Stallion bartender Peter Roy) flew off the jump locked inside a refrigerator. He survived and became a lawyer (in real estate, not personal injury).

After a few years, the jump was dismantled when insurance companies put the nix on high school and college ski jumping.

Interlude

JUD STRUNK, VALLEY BALLADEER

Among the songs the Apollo 17 astronauts brought to the moon in December 1972 was a new tune written and sung by an alumnus of the Red Stallion stage. "Daisy a Day," Jud Strunk's sweet ballad of everlasting love, was on its way to becoming a Billboard country and pop-music hit, and Strunk had recently made his debut as a cast member on the country's most popular television show, the vaudeville-for-the-hippie-era

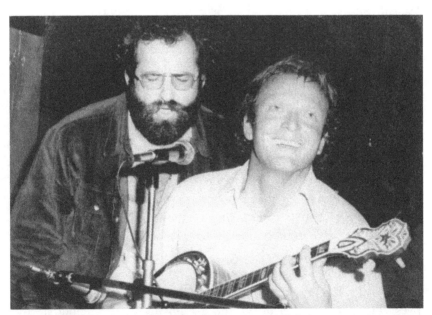

Jud Strunk (right) with his frequent band companion Al Scheeren.
COURTESY OF JEFF STRUNK

program *Laugh-In*. Had he not been killed in a plane crash near Sugarloaf Regional Airport in 1981, perhaps Strunk would have joined fellow *Laugh-In* cast members Goldie Hawn and Lily Tomlin in decades-long celebrity. Perhaps. One reason Strunk was living back where his career began is that national demand for his acts had waned. The other reason, the main reason, is that he loved it there.

Singer, songwriter, banjoist, tap dancer, spoon player, and homespun humorist, Strunk had entertained people since his childhood in upstate New York. In 1960, when he was twenty-four, he was cast as a banjo player in the off-Broadway play *Beautiful Dreamer*, featuring the music of Stephen Foster. Two years later, he followed his passion for skiing to western Maine, where he and his wife, Marti, made their home in Sugarloaf Village, where he was hired to sell house lots. He also worked in public relations for Sugarloaf.

With bass fiddler Billy Jones and pianist Ed Krause, Strunk made his local debut at the opening of the Red Stallion Inn on New Year's Day 1962. After that, Strunk-led ensembles blending folk music and Will Rogers–style humor and social commentary became mainstays of Sugarloaf's après-ski scene. The best known was the Carrabassett Grange Hall Talent Contest–Winning Band (a.k.a. the Sugarloafers), composed of Strunk, Al Scheeren, Billy Jones, John McCafferty, and Icky Webber. Sugarloaf hired the band to promote New England skiing at ski shows and festivals around the country, which led to Strunk accepting a job out west performing at fundraisers for the U.S. Ski Team.

"I don't mind saying I miss Maine," he wrote in a letter published in the *Bangor Daily News* in March 1965. "We have settled in Denver, and my wife, Marti, and the family seem well pleased. No birches, spruce, and pine, however I know I'm going to yearn to get out the smelting net when the time comes up shortly this spring. I hope to be in the Northeast soon, and that I'll be able to drop over at Sugarloaf and spend some time with the world's greatest people."

Strunk's musicianship, lyrics about the denizens of Maine small towns, and folksy humor attracted the attention of TV network executives. "He had a wonderful ear and a forgiving way of telling stories," Scheeren told the *Original Irregular* in 1985. After two appearances on

Jud Strunk, flanked by Bill Jones (left) and Al Scheeren.
COURTESY OF SUGARLOAF SKI CLUB

The Merv Griffin Show in 1968, Strunk and his family moved to California to boost his career. He toured with the Andy Williams Road Show, sang with Petula Clark, and was cast in small roles on *Bewitched* episodes set in Salem, Massachusetts, once as a maitre d' and once as a bell boy. He released his debut album, *Downeast Viewpoint*, in 1970, followed by *Jones' General Store* in 1971.

In August 1972, ABC-TV gave Strunk his own hour-long special. A month later, he made his debut on *Laugh-In*, on which he had recurring roles as a hayseed sportscaster delivering the news from Kingfield, Maine, and as "Frank Farkel's friend" whose "father's father, Fred, was a first-family founding father of Farmington and one of the few farmers who fed his flocks and fertilized his fields with Frank Faulkner's famous fodder." Just a couple months into his *Laugh-In* gig, Strunk and his Carrabassett Grange Hall Talent Contest–Winning Band performed on *Hee Haw*, a *Laugh-In* copycat for country-music fans. The band members' unpretentiousness and laidback style made an impression. "I was amazed at the response for a crazy bunch of rough-cuts," Al Scheeren said. "But things were always rough-cut for Jud."

By this time, Strunk was building a log home on one hundred acres in Eustis, and in an interview with the *Chicago Tribune*, he made it clear that he considered Maine, not California, his home. "I don't believe there is anyone in Los Angeles who could buy here what I have in Maine," he said.

The sentimentality of "Daisy a Day" made it an unusual hit for Strunk, whose other chart toppers were playful and a bit suggestive, like "The Biggest Parakeets in Town" and "Pamela Brown." "Daisy" offers a glimpse at a facet of Strunk's personality that only his family and close friends saw. "He could have 1,000 people holding their sides from laughing so hard, and then go backstage and burst into tears over something personal that was troubling him," Marguerite Robichaux, Strunk's partner after his divorce, told the *Irregular*. "He was a master at moving people's emotions, maybe because he found it so easy himself to be moved to tears or laughter."

Robichaux's observations echoed those shared by *Morning Sentinel* reporter Ann McGowan a few days after Strunk's death. "He wasn't just a writer of poems, or a writer of songs, or a singer, or a banjo player, or a Maine humorist," McGowan said. "He was all of those things and more. He was an entertainer who evoked emotions."

Strunk concerts drew big crowds in Maine up until his death. He appeared in benefit performances for a variety of groups, favoring those with an environmental mission, like FOIL, which formed in 1975 to keep oil refineries out of Maine. He opened a restaurant in his home, performing on banjo while Robichaux cooked and his three sons waited tables. His friends helped build the kitchen and deliver seafood. Dick Ayotte, the owner of Ayotte's General Store, took reservations.

Ayotte was at Strunk's side when he decided to take his newly restored 1941 Fairchild M62-A plane for spin on October 5, 1981. Strunk suffered a heart attack shortly after takeoff from Sugarloaf Regional Airport. The plane rolled and crashed, killing both men. Strunk was forty-five, Ayotte forty-three.

Four decades after his death, Strunk is still a presence in Carrabassett Valley. His son Jeff is a co-owner of the Rack restaurant and bar, where his grandson, Mason, performs his songs.

8

Whiskey Valley

ON NEW YEAR'S EVE IN 1968, A TWENTY-YEAR-OLD ACCOUNTANT
named Larry Warren left his office in Boston and drove north, destination Sugarloaf/USA. A novice skier, he'd studied ski-area maps before
settling on Sugarloaf for his first big-mountain escapade. It had what
he was looking for: adrenaline-pumping slopes and, nearby, one of New
England's liveliest ski-town nightspots, a converted barn called the Red
Stallion Inn, where he'd booked a room for the week.

The Red Stallion in the early 1960s. COURTESY OF JAY AND WENDY WYMAN

When Warren pulled into the Stallion's snow-packed parking lot four hours later, it was dark, snow was falling, and temps were in the low 20s, but the barn's windows were wide open, blaring rock music and expelling cigarette smoke. (Open windows, Warren would learn, were the Stallion's ventilation system, no matter the season.) Just inside the entrance, Warren told the young guy collecting cover charges that he had a room reservation. "Let me get my brother," the kid said, and he disappeared into the crowded bar.

A few minutes later, another young man appeared. Shifting the toothpick balanced on his lip, he introduced himself as Ed Rogers and invited Warren into his office. "We're looking forward to your stay here this week," he said, "but tonight we've got a little problem."

"Oh, yeah?" Warren said warily.

"We're overbooked. We don't have a room for you." But if Warren didn't mind, Rogers quickly continued, he could sleep in the women's bunkroom, free of charge.

The Sound Track performs at the Red Stallion. COURTESY OF JAY AND WENDY WYMAN

John Rogers took this photo of the Red Stallion in 1966, the year he and wife Caroline bought it. Under their sons' management, the Red Stallion's rowdy reputation grew. COURTESY OF PETER AND JANE ROY

Warren didn't mind (he was twenty, remember). Rogers then escorted him into the dining room and introduced him to the bartenders and the waitstaff, who were told to give him all the free drinks he wanted and a free steak dinner too, and to the hat-haired, jeans-clad regulars drinking beer and throwing quarters across the back bar into the tip bucket—a black bed-pan affixed to the wall. The room vibrated to the thumping music; the small sunken dance floor bounced under gyrating feet. "I thought, 'This place is nuts!'" Warren, the visionary behind several Carrabassett-area institutions including the Sugarloaf Golf Club and Maine Huts & Trails, recalled many years later. "Everybody was happy and loose, open and friendly. I couldn't imagine going into a hotel and being treated like that. I loved it."

MISBEHAVING AND ACTING BADLY

Sugarloafers of the 1960s and early 1970s had a nickname for their woodsy retreat: Whiskey Valley. It encapsulated their enthusiasm for their favorite activities by day ("we ski") and night (no explanation needed), as well as the buoyant anarchy that prevailed in their settlement. As unorganized townships, Jerusalem and Crockertown were essentially lawless. There were no select boards to impose ordinances, no codes officers to issue citations, and no local cops to patrol Route 27. Residents remember interacting with two state troopers—one who cruised the beat for many years and the young academy grad who briefly replaced him—before State Trooper Ron Moody arrived. Moody had an avuncular enforcement style, according to former Red Stallion waitress Meg Rogers, who remembered him striding through the bar and pointing to the most inebriated revelers: "You're not driving . . . you're not driving . . . you're not driving."[40] Moody, who became Carrabassett Valley's first police chief in 1988 and created

The Carrabassett Grange Hall Talent Contest–Winning Band (a.k.a. the Sugarloafers) was a mainstay of the 1960s scene. From left: Al Scheeren, Billy Jones, Jud Strunk, and John McCafferty. COURTESY OF JEFF STRUNK

40. At the time she worked at the Stallion, Meg was married to Dave Hutchinson. She later married Ed Rogers's brother Frank.

its blended town-resort police force, later told the *Daily Bulldog* that he'd been more of a guardian than a disciplinarian. "Arrest isn't my philosophy," he said. He traced his approach to the advice given him when he was a nineteen-year-old rookie in Ogunquit: "We're in the resort business," the chief had told him on his first day. "We're here to take care of people."

Despite all the construction that had taken place over the twenty years since the Bigelow Boys cut their first trail, Carrabassett Valley still felt like the middle of nowhere, particularly to city dwellers like New York *Daily News* reporter Jerry Kenney. When he visited in 1969, Kenney felt he'd stumbled on a ski-country Brigadoon with mysterious magnetic charms. "Skiers have been known to come here for a season finale and never be heard from again by the outside world," he said. "The lure of Sugarloaf alone is powerful enough, but coupled with life in the valley, its inhabitants and their mores, it's almost overpowering. . . . After dark, that's when the lure of Carrabassett Valley really gets to the visitor. Following dinner, there never was much to do except listen to the local people talk fishing or hunting. Or if one could find where Jud Strunk was plinking his banjo and reciting Carrabassett verse, they'd flock around."

The après-ski scene may have been small, but the young clientele's enthusiasm for partying was huge and unabashed—the inspiration, in fact, behind the name of the Bag restaurant and bar (everyone was "half in the bag"—get it?). The Bag's proprietors, Billy Jones and Icky Webber, even gave their friends keys to the back door so they could grab beers on Sundays when Maine's blue laws prohibited stores from selling alcohol.

Jones, who'd grown up in Eustis and had been working at or around Sugarloaf since he was a fifteen-year-old flipping burgers in the base lodge, played bass fiddle in Jud Strunk's popular folk ensemble, the Sugarloafers (a.k.a. the Carrabassett Grange Hall Talent Contest–Winning Band). That made him an especially valuable member of the Bad Actors comedy troupe. The group's instigator was Philip "Brud" Folger, a University of Maine ski team coach, who said he and his friends would come off the mountain after a day of skiing and say to each other, "What are we gonna do?" followed by "I don't know," followed by drinking at one of the local bars. One night in 1967, over beers at the Capricorn Lodge, Folger told his friends about his junior year abroad in Austria and how

Dead River Company's 1968 calendar featured this photo of a crane-loading operation in Jerusalem Township. Herb Dickey, a Dead River Company forester in the 1970s, rescued several calendars that were destined for the trash when the company gutted and renovated its headquarters. COURTESY OF HERB DICKEY

everyone would gather in a hotel bar to watch the ski instructors put on shows with yodeling, guitar playing, singing, and dancing. Inspired, the party retreated to Bigelow Station, the Folger family's camp, and concocted several skits to perform as an opening act for the Sugarloafers, thus guaranteeing they'd have an audience. Exactly which of the newly founded Bad Actors was there that first night varies with the storyteller, but the cast ultimately came to include Brud Folger, Icky Webber, Parker Hall, Dave Hutchinson, Ted Jones, Carl "Dutch" Demshar, Billy Jones, Jud Strunk, and Al Scheeren.

The Bad Actors were a top après-ski attraction for six or seven years, most often performing at the Capricorn Lodge, which had the best space for their antics, not to mention a bartender who rewarded them with a better-quality bourbon than what they received at other venues. Exuberantly unrefined, the Bad Actors had no ambitions beyond the valley; they were content to be silly in front of an audience of friends. Their

A lumber truck is seen at Poplar Stream Falls in the Dead River Company's 1969 calendar. COURTESY OF HERB DICKEY

signature routine featured four barflies puzzling over a minute object that they passed among themselves fingertip to fingertip, until one of them revealed he'd found it in his nose. "We started every performance, if you want to call it that, with bourbon and a couple cases of beer," said Demshar, a former Brunswick Naval Air Station pilot who settled in the valley in 1968 and eventually became one of the area's most prolific building contractors. "Most of the time, I was the light man. Each person who was participating in a skit would go on stage, and when he was ready, I'd turn on the light. They'd do their monologue or joke or whatever it was, and then I'd turn the light off. It was very quick. The average show had about 25 jokes, some of them relatively risqué, most not."[41]

THE RED STALLION

By far the rowdiest bar in the valley, the Red Stallion served its first cocktail at 12:01 a.m. on January 1, 1962, according to a written remembrance

---

41. Carl Demshar shared his knowledge of Carrabassett Valley history in 2021. He died in the fall of 2022.

by Dave Rollins, who converted the former Dead River horse barn into a restaurant and hostelry with his business partner, Wes Sanborn. Staff members Florence Hall and Laura Dunham designed the renovation: Just inside the front door was a small lobby with an office to the left and a bunkroom to the right (some years later, the bunkroom was refashioned into "the little bar"). A staircase led to pine-paneled guest rooms in the former hayloft. Straight ahead was the super-rustic dining room, with booths around the edges and a bar against the back wall. The dance area sat a few inches below the tile-red softwood floor; local legend holds its notorious springiness was due to its resting on a bed of horse manure, but more likely the dance floor bounced because it was built on beams instead of a solid foundation, according to Ed Rogers. Rogers didn't deny, however, that the dining room sometimes had an *eau de barnyard*, particularly during heavy rain.

On stage that New Year's morning in 1962 were Jud Strunk, Billy Jones, and pianist Ed Krause. Strunk, then twenty-six and a recent transplant to the area from upstate New York, went on to form what was for a time the Stallion's de facto house band with trombonist Bob Marden, clarinetist Dick Dubord, and trumpeter Fred Petra. "Often impromptu, Dick Dubord and Jud Strunk brought the house down with their stand-up comedy routines," Rollins writes. "The Stallion was a wild and woolly place, but usually under control because Florence Hall and Laura Dunham commanded great respect from the regulars—a combination of local Jud Strunk fans, Sugarloaf staff, and skiers."

It became wilder and woollier when the Rogers family took over in 1966. The business was in foreclosure after its second owner, John Love, had been unable to make the mortgage payments, and Ed convinced his father to take out a bank loan to acquire it. Ed was determined to turn the Stallion into a nightspot on par with Killington's Wobbly Barn and Sugarbush's Blue Tooth. Dinner hour at the Stallion was wholesome, especially on Thursdays when two-for-one specials were a big draw, but as the evening progressed, the families cleared out and the ski bums moved in, transforming the dining room into a nightclub that had a New England–wide reputation for hosting great bands. "I kept trying to push the limit of making the Red Stallion *the* place to go—getting bands and the whole

Larry and Gail Warren in 2018. Larry is the instigator behind such institutions as the Sugarloaf Golf Club, Maine Huts & Trails, and even the Carrabassett Valley Sanitary District and its Snowfluent. COURTESY OF DAVE COTA

works," Rogers said. "And it worked. We had monster crowds right from the start. I always was jealous if we didn't have the most people staying at our hotel and the most people at my bar at night." Overbooking rooms was so common that staff joked that when guests arrived, they'd find Ed so he could introduce them to the couple they'd be sleeping with.

Rogers hired a Pittsfield band, the Missing Links, to play most weekends, and its trumpeter and pianist, Leon Southard, sometimes performed through the week. The most popular band, at least among the Stallion's female patrons, was Molly McGregor, according to Meg Rogers. The long-haired lead singer, Hank Castonguay, started each set writhing under a blanket on the floor of the darkened stage. When the music kicked up and the lights flashed on, he'd leap to his feet, wearing less clothing than he'd had during the previous set. By evening's end, he'd be clad in only a leather jockstrap.

The Stallion's management team included Ed's wife, Wendy, and his brothers, Frank and Bob (it was Bob who was collecting covers on the night of Larry Warren's first visit). Each of the male staff members was known to regulars by his nickname—Captain America (Peter Roy), the Rooster (John Corcoran), the General (Terry Snow), White Trash (Mike Sheridan), and Groovy Garbage (Jim Nickerson), to name a few. The crew continually cooked up causes to party around, like the Miss Ayotte Country Store Pageant and, during one snow-poor winter, Beach Week, when a load of sand was piled in the dining room.

The Red Stallion's reputation for barely contained chaos belied its role as an incubator for on-mountain and valley-wide projects. It's where Ed Rogers, David Rolfe, and Harry Baxter dreamed up Sugarloaf competitions like Horror Week, during which the Stallion staff proudly skied

1968

$100 DOWN—$25 per month. Large lots near Sugarloaf ski area. Electricity, telephone, and water at property. $995. Call 282-xxxx. —*Biddeford-Saco Journal,* January 10

1968

Officials at Sugarloaf closed the resort to skiing after a 30-below reading was reported at the gondola mid-station early Monday, with winds gusting to 55 miles an hour. Amos Winter—despite his name, he had nothing to do with the weather—said he can't remember a day colder than Monday. —*Bangor Daily News*, January 9

in white coveralls emblazoned with the words *Red Stallion Horror Team*. Rogers launched the *Irregular* newspaper in 1967 out of the Red Stallion dining room, with Liz Hall as its first editor and, a year or two later, Rolfe as its first full-time publisher. Rogers also led the Sugarloaf Area Association as it created a central phone number for booking lodging and organized events like White White World, a weeklong costume party across several venues that culminated with the crowning of a Sugarloaf king and queen. His most significant accomplishment was founding the North America Pro Ski Tour, which evolved into the World Pro Ski Tour.

"THIS IS GOING TO BE FUN"

The morning after his stay in the women's bunkroom, Larry Warren took a lesson with Sugarloaf ski school instructor Dick Allison. "His approach to teaching was to take me to the top of the mountain and go down the Narrow Gauge and over the head wall, then just stay on the number three T-bar and the hardest part of the mountain all day long," Warren said. "I crashed and burned and tumbled. By the end of the day, I made one run over the head wall without falling. He said, 'There! If you can do that, you can do anything!'" Warren went back to the Stallion for more steaks and beer and dancing. That was his routine for the rest of the week.

After that, he spent weekend after weekend at the Stallion. He became friends with the Rogerses, the bartenders, and the regulars, including businesspeople from around Maine who had camps in the valley. In January 1970, one of them, Portland-based accountant (and

Getting Trashed

Typically one had to be female and naked to occupy a spread in *Playboy* in the 1960s. But in November 1969, the editors of the magazine that helped usher in the sexual revolution devoted a two-pager to some hell-raisers in wool hats and puffy jackets dancing atop trash and mud in the Maine woods. With that, the first Carrabassett Dump Party became a symbol of Sugarloaf's legendary party era.

That was the idea. In March 1969, word got around that a *Playboy* writer was coming to Sugarloaf to research a feature on eastern ski areas. Eager to demonstrate the valley's partying prowess, David Rolfe, publisher of the *Sugarloaf Irregular* and event coordinator for Sugarloaf Area Association, proposed a bash on the Carriage Road hillside where camp and business owners had been tossing their trash, old appliances, and assorted detritus for years. Most of the planning took place at the Red Stallion, of course, and most of the partiers were Red Stallion regulars.

Courtney Knapp, Carrabassett Valley's longtime fire chief, was a member of Crimson Tide, the high school band from Phillips hired to play. Seeing people drink, dance, and ride an old refrigerator downhill made a lasting impression. "As teenagers, we'd never been exposed to the after-hours activities here in the valley, but we knew about the Red Stallion—it had a lot of notoriety," he said.

One or two more dump parties followed, but Don Fowler said they failed to live up to the original. "They tried to charge admission and commercialize it, which wasn't any fun," he said. "Then they closed the dump, and the whole thing went away."

A video of the second dump party, in 1970, can be seen on the WSKI website, wskitv.com.

1970

An electrical power failure at 12:40 Saturday at Sugarloaf nearly ignited a riot. More than 1,000 skiers, many in Maine for school vacation holidays, stormed Sugarloaf's main lodge and demanded their lift money refunded. "We returned $1,036 in lift money and lord only knows how many held onto their tickets and will use them again as rain checks," general manager Harry Baxter said. The blackout, according to the Rangeley Power and Electric Co., came when two fuses in a transformer burned out in the area of Route 27 and the access road. —*Bangor Daily News*, March 2

future Carrabassett Valley selectman) Alden Macdonald, offered him a job working with one of his biggest clients—Sugarloaf. Warren accepted, but within a few months Sugarloaf general manager Charlie Skinner hired him, with Macdonald's blessing, to replace Ted Jones as comptroller (Jones left to start a woodworking business).

After work, Warren often went to the Red Stallion to drink beer and play cribbage. "It was like the local gossip center, like going to the hairdresser," he said. One afternoon in 1971, he and his friends—Ed Rogers, David Rolfe, Ted Jones, and the soon-to-be founders of Tufulio's Restaurant, Joe Williamson and Larry Sullivan—got into an animated conversation about Chris Hutchins's crazy idea for getting out from under LURC's jurisdiction. Warren remembered their excitement building as they considered the benefits of creating their own town: "We'd keep our tax money instead of sending it to the state . . . the world will be our oyster . . . we can do some wild and crazy things . . . hey, this going to be fun!"

Household Names

In 1968, the *Bangor Daily News* reported more than seven hundred chalets, log cabins, and A-frames around Sugarloaf. Owners were from all over Maine, as well as forty Massachusetts cities and towns; the states of Connecticut, New Hampshire, New York, Rhode Island, Virginia, Pennsylvania, and New Jersey; and the provinces of Quebec and Newfoundland. Many dwellings sported signs with playful names. Among them:

Bean Pot (Paul Bean, Melrose, Massachusetts)

Bigeloaf (Horton Gilman, Gorham)

Bigelow Bungalow (John Tiernan, Presque Isle)

Bit o' Sugar (Willard McLaughlin, Houlton)

Carrabassett Asset (Paul Holliday, Scarsdale, New York)

Chateau de Coop (Thurlow Cooper, Portland)

Crockerbox (Dr. William Kierstead, Waterville)

Kissing' Cousins (Howard Cousins, Bangor)

The National Debt (Alden Macdonald, Portland)

Scotts on the Rocks (Sheldon Scott, Caribou)

Sno-dunder (Richard Bell, Farmington)

Sugarlump (E. J. Gilman, Cape Elizabeth)

Sugarplum (Jim Libby, South Portland)

Sugarshack (Roland Nadeau, Rochester, New Hampshire)

Trollheim (Helen Caldwell Cushman, Mount Vernon)

Interlude

MOUNTAINS OUT OF VOLE HILLS

The denizens of Carrabassett Valley took their responsibility for the yellow-nosed vole very seriously, as this bumper sticker attests. COURTESY OF NICK KARAHALIOS

From the Legislative Record of May 2, 1975.

Out of order and under suspension of the rules, the Senate voted to take up the following joint resolution:

Mr. [Neal] Corson of Somerset presents the following Joint Resolution and moves its adoption:

WHEREAS, the Sugarloaf Mountain Corporation is constructing a double chairlift and related ski access trails on Sugarloaf Mountain in Franklin County; and

WHEREAS, Sugarloaf Mountain is one of three known locations in Maine where the yellow-nosed vole lives; and

WHEREAS, the yellow-nosed vole *(Microtus chrotorrhinus)* is one of the world's rarest and least-known mammals and is on the Inland Fisheries and Game Department's unofficial list of potentially endangered wildlife in Maine; and

WHEREAS, the yellow-nosed vole does not like to cross grassy areas, which are the habitat of its competitor, the red-backed vole; and

WHEREAS, the Sugarloaf Mountain Corporation has agreed to plant trefoil beneath the chairlift to encourage the yellow-nosed vole to cross this area in their multitudinous journeys from wood to wood now, therefore, be it

RESOLVED, that we, the members of the 107th Legislature in regular session, do hereby respectfully urge and request the Department of Inland Fisheries and Game to place no less than three, nor no more than six, signs along the chairlift, these signs to read "Warning, Vole Crossing" and to be of sufficient size to be clearly visible to persons utilizing the chairlift; and be it further

RESOLVED, that the Secretary of the Senate shall send a suitable copy of this resolution to Maynard F. Marsh, commissioner of Inland Fisheries and Game.

The PRESIDENT: The Chair recognizes the senator from Somerset, Senator Corson.

Mr. CORSON: Mr. President, Distinguished Members of the Senate: On the 21st day of March, 1975, the Land Use Regulation Commission issued to Sugarloaf Corporation the development permit for the chairlift mentioned in the Joint Resolution.

When I first saw a copy of the permit, I thought it was joke, a caricature of the method of operation in which LURC seems to delight. But, to my great surprise, it is authentic.

I now quote from the permit: "The Department of Inland Fisheries and Game makes the following recommendations:

"This proposed development activity could have a potentially severe effect on local wildlife populations. Sugarloaf Mountain is one of three known locations in Maine where the yellow-nosed vole lives. This is one of the world's rarest and least known mammals. It is on the Inland Fisheries and Game Department's unofficial list of potentially endangered wildlife in Maine.

"The yellow-nosed vole lives in the Canadian life zone which in Maine is found only at higher elevations. Construction activity at these higher elevations may destroy valuable habitat and the alteration of remaining areas for ski trails may make the habitat more suitable for meadow voles, a competitor of the yellow-nosed vole."

Mr. President. I confess that when I first saw this permit, I was not overly familiar with the yellow-nosed vole. But I have been doing some research on this matter, and I would like to share with my colleagues the results of my work. I am quoting now from an article by Dr. Robert L. Martin, world renowned expert on the yellow-nosed vole.

"This robust-bodied, short-tailed mouse looks much like the common meadow mouse, a close relative, except for its yellowish nose and a different pattern of the molar teeth. Known from the mountains of North Carolina to Labrador, they have generally been taken at elevations above 3,000 feet.

"Like the Labrador collared lemming, this vole tends to retain its feces and establish sanitary stations on the surface, whereas most other mice native to the Northeast tend to drop their fecal pellets at random."

Dr. Martin goes on to note that "a sanitary station, when located, provides a good trapping site for catching one of these rare mice—somewhat akin to booby-trapping the path to the back-house."

It was stated in the permit that there are only three known locations in Maine where the yellow-nosed vole lives. It was noted at the hearing on this permit application that the vole hunters had only looked in three locations in Maine. And one of the reasons they looked on Sugarloaf is that they are allowed to ride the gondola free of charge.

It was stated that the yellow-nosed vole is on the unofficial list of potentially endangered mammals.

Mr. President, I submit that all life on this planet is potentially endangered, with the possible exception of the blackfly.

It was stated that the red-backed vole is a competitor of the yellow-nosed vole. Mr. Billings of LURC requested clarification of this statement. He asked if the red-backed voles and the yellow-nosed voles fight each other. Dr. Martin informed him that they do not, but if they did, the yellow-nosed voles would win as they are very aggressive and the red-backed voles are very passive.

The permit went on to state that "prior to the commencement of clearing or construction, members of the Land Use Regulation Commission staff, Department of Inland Fisheries and Game, and Sugarloaf Mountain Corporation representatives shall meet and draw up a management plan having the following objectives:

a.) to maintain, protect, or improve in perpetuity, the alpine habitat of the yellow-nosed vole; and

b.) to provide a reasonable economic return to the landowner."

Very kind of LURC to allow a business to make a reasonable economic return, although what concern that is of LURC's I don't understand. That meeting has taken place, and Sugarloaf has agreed to plant trefoil, which yellow-nosed voles like and red-backed voles hate. The problem appears to have been solved to the satisfaction of all concerned, although to my mind, the problem should never have arisen in the first place. It is just such action as this LURC permit that causes the good citizens of Maine to despair of ever finding reason and common sense in dealings with their government.

LURC has often demonstrated its ability to make a mountain out of a molehill. I submit that LURC has reached new heights of sublime inanity. The Land Use Regulation Commission has finally succeeded in making a vole hill out of a mountain.

Mr. President, I move the passage of this Joint Resolution.

The PRESIDENT: Is it now the pleasure of the Senate that this Joint Resolution be adopted and sent down for concurrence.

The motion prevailed.

9

Who Do We Want to Be?

CONVERSATIONS ABOUT FORMING A TOWN TOOK PLACE THROUGHOUT the valley in the months following the March 1971 organization meeting. In April, the state legislature passed an act to incorporate the town of Carrabassett Valley and directed the secretary of state to call a referendum in Jerusalem, the only township in which the proposal had clear momentum. Wyman's three registered voters, in fact, had given the proposal a unanimous thumbs down in the March straw poll. Sugarloaf's thirteen voters had split 7–6 against. Now a study committee was gathering information on the opportunities and challenges of self-governance.

A Nordic ski touring center, owned by Carrabassett Valley and managed by Sugarloaf, was the new town's first major project. COURTESY OF JAMIE WALTER

With just one vote to flip in Sugarloaf, proponents lobbied Norton Luce, in part because Jean, a study committee member, favored incorporation. Plus, Norton's opinion carried weight. His Sugarloaf Village neighbors fondly called him "the mayor"—he was their go-to guy for information about the region and the resort, and, because he owned the valley's only heating business, they literally trusted him with the keys to their homes.

Like everyone else, Norton was unhappy about high property taxes. However, his family had been active in Farmington government for generations, and he knew it was a complicated and challenging business. He didn't think there were enough people living in the valley to run a town, never mind enough with the maturity and experience to do it competently. After all, most of them were ski bums who spent their days racing down the mountain and their nights imbibing or slinging drinks.

Preston Jordan and Larry Warren, among others, did their best to sell the idea to Norton. Besides lowering property taxes, they said, the new town would derive income from a trust fund set up from taxes paid over the past one hundred years by Jerusalem citizens. It could take advantage of federal and state programs for local governments and do its own land-use planning. Of course, they argued, the biggest benefit was that residents would govern themselves. Nevertheless, after two subsequent public meetings at which these points were further expounded, Norton held firm. Once again, Sugarloaf voted 7–6 against incorporation, and Wyman's residents remained unanimous in their opposition.

So on October 26, 1971, thirty-four Jerusalem registered voters marched into Judson's Motel to vote in a referendum overseen by Deputy Secretary of State Peter Damborg. Red Stallion Inn co-owner Frank Rogers cast the first paper ballot. By a vote of 21–13, the town of Carrabassett Valley was born.

A TOWN WITHOUT HANG-UPS

The town's incorporation became official on March 15, 1972, a serendipitous one year after Chris Hutchins made his first formal pitch on the benefits of self-government. That evening, the first town meeting convened

Carrabassett Valley's trails are consistently ranked among the best skiing and mountain biking facilities in the Northeast. COURTESY OF JAMIE WALTER

Sugarloaf maintains and grooms trails around the town-owned Outdoor Center.
SAMUEL TRAFTON/MAINE DRONE IMAGING

in a room above Ayotte's Country Store in Dead River Company's Valley Crossing Shopping Center. The agenda was narrowly focused on setting up the new government. Voters elected Preston Jordan as first selectman and Larry Warren and Parker Hall as selectmen. Shirley Smith, Gail Jordan, and Martha Ayotte composed the school committee. Maralyn Beck was appointed town clerk, tax collector, and treasurer. Finally, voters enacted an ordinance to establish a planning board, opting out of being regulated by LURC. Because the new town had so few residents, nonresident property owners were authorized to serve on various boards.

Larry Warren took the lead in formulating a budget. The town had little taxable value, he said, but its expenses were "next to nothing." There were no schools, and all the subdivision roads were maintained by home-owner associations, leaving just a two-and-a-half-mile stretch of Long Falls Dam Road for the town to maintain and plow. Voters returned to

Valley Crossing Shopping Center on April 26 and approved a $24,125 budget, the biggest chunk of which was $6,560 in municipal operating expenses, followed by $5,697 for tuition and transportation of the town's four schoolchildren to School Administrative District 58 (Phillips, Avon, Kingfield, and Strong). With that, property taxes dropped 66 percent.

The creation of a town in which only forty-five people lived and a lumber company turned real-estate developer owned 90 percent of the land drew the skeptical attention of the *Maine Sunday Telegram* in August. Reporter Lloyd Ferris paraphrased unnamed "cynics, most of them in key environmental watchdog positions," who believed the town had been created primarily for the benefit of Dead River Company so it could mold land-use planning "along lines friendly to its own costly development projects." Chris Hutchins, however, insisted that Dead River hadn't—and wouldn't—interfere in town affairs. "I am confident that Carrabassett Valley will adopt, if not identical guidelines, stronger language than LURC's," he told Ferris.

"I don't think we've ever made a decision in which the Dead River Company influenced our vote at all," Parker Hall agreed. "They come secondary in any planning." Besides, the thirty-four-year-old selectman suggested, the *Telegram* was missing the real story: "Our town is a very rare kind of town in that it is made up of brand-new transients who have come here from other places. We're composed almost entirely of young people with about 90 percent of our voters between the ages of 25 and 35. We're going to make this a model town."

Planning board member Ed Rogers, then thirty-two, likewise emphasized youthful leaders, whose fresh, energetic ideas were unhampered by stale, ingrained protocols. "Carrabassett Valley is a rich town controlled by people who are able to do pretty much what they want to do without the hang-ups you usually find in most towns," he said. "We are able to determine our own destiny."

FUN IS OUR INDUSTRIAL PARK

One of the new town's first orders of business was to write a zoning ordinance and create a planning board. "As we started setting all this stuff up, we could see that we needed to identify a mission and a path forward,"

The golf course was Carrabassett Valley and Sugarloaf's second project together.
COURTESY OF JAMIE WALTER

Warren said. Noting that there were only a handful of year-round jobs in the town, the select board prioritized creating sustainable employment opportunities. That meant, as Warren put it, "figuring out what it is we want this town to be."

They believed the answer lay in developing the area's recreation-based economy. They were particularly interested in the potential of the one-thousand-acre public lot that had passed from state to town ownership when Carrabassett Valley incorporated.

Public lots, or public reserved lands, are a legacy dating to colonial times. When Massachusetts was selling large tracts of land to men like William Bingham, it set aside 1,000–1,200-acre lots in nearly every township—about four hundred thousand acres in all—to be used to raise funds for public schools and the ministry. If a lumber company owned a township and logged trees on the public lot, for example, it would pay a percentage of its profit to the Maine Forest Service, which would then deposit it into the trust fund.[42]

---

42. After Maine became a state, religion was dropped as a beneficiary, and the trusts were to be used solely for schools.

That was how the system was supposed to work, anyway. In 1972, the *Maine Sunday Telegram* published a series of reports detailing how the state forestry department had been mismanaging public lands by selling off rights to harvest trees for "as little as a nickel an acre" and spending much of the revenue from those transactions instead of putting it into trust funds. "The value [of the lots] today is not in the timber harvesting potential that the state sold," reporter Bob Cummings wrote. "Maine already grows twice as much wood each year as its mills can use. The shortage is in public recreation. . . . Aside from the occasional leasing of camp lots, Maine has largely ignored the recreational value of its vast domain." That situation was changing, though. Governor Kenneth M. Curtis had issued an executive order setting up a joint committee of state department heads to coordinate plans for acquiring lands for recreation, conservation, and open space preservation.

Cummings's first article was published on March 13, 1972—two days before Carrabassett Valley's first town meeting—and the controversy simmered in the press and in Augusta for months. In one article, Cummings shared speculation that Carrabassett Valley residents, "mainly employees of the ski area, will sell the lot and use the proceeds for après-ski parties."

The controversy culminated in the creation of the Bureau of Public Lands (BPL) in October 1973 and a change in law: No longer would a township acquire a public lot when it incorporated the way Carrabassett Valley had. Instead, the state would retain ownership and take back rights to the tract's "timber, grass, and growth."

BPL's director was Richard Barringer, the author of *A Maine Manifest*, which, among other things, advocated for the formation of a public land bank to protect traditional access to Maine's fields, forests, and waters from privatization. Larry Warren had devoured the book and believed Barringer would be open to the development of a recreation area on both Carrabassett Valley's public lot and the abutting state-owned 1,200-acre public lot in Sugarloaf Township, which was now under BPL's jurisdiction. He reached out to Barringer, and he was correct: the idea was right up the director's alley. Not long after, town and state partnered to hire Peter Berg and Associates, a Vermont land-planning firm, to study ways that the combined tracts—2,100 acres, or 3.3 square miles in all—could be developed for the benefit of Maine people.

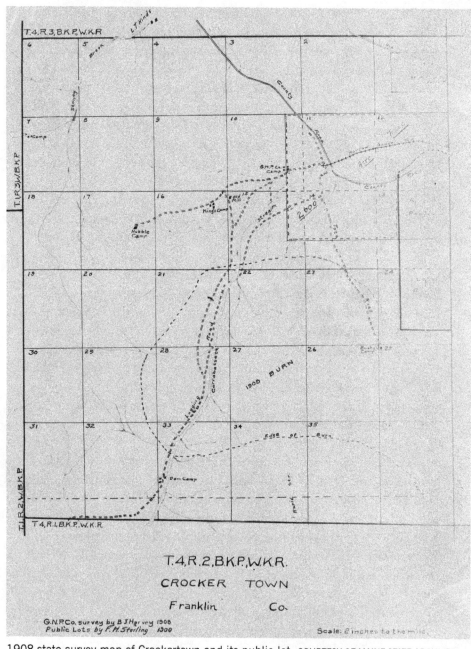

1908 state survey map of Crockertown and its public lot. COURTESY OF MAINE STATE ARCHIVES

Up in Sugarloaf Township, residents were impressed—and surprised—by what those ski bums in the valley were doing. They'd seen Carrabassett Valley transition to a town-manager government, with a mature and experienced businessman, forty-nine-year-old Preston Jordon, at the helm. They were especially envious of Carrabassett Valley's low tax rate—8.3 mills compared to the township's 21.75. Now, with excitement building over the public lots, some were rethinking their earlier position on forming a town. In January 1975, Sugarloaf property owners went to the polls to decide whether to start the process of being annexed to Carrabassett Valley. The number of voters was thirteen, just as it was in 1971. And just as it was in 1971, the vote split 7–6, only this time the measure passed. Norton Luce had changed his mind.

State senator Neal Corson introduced emergency legislation to authorize the merger so that Sugarloaf residents would see a reduction in their 1975 tax bills. The act passed in late February. Two weeks later, both communities weighed in one more time: Sugarloaf's voters approved annexation 29–0; Carrabassett Valley agreed to accept the township by a vote of 50–8. The newly expanded town had a population of just over one hundred people, including twenty-one schoolchildren. Its state valuation was $13,812,000, much of it attributed to the ski area and to the 123 condominiums that had been built at Sugarloaf since 1970.

The expanded municipality's first town meeting was held March 26 in the base lodge. Residents decided to stick with the name Carrabassett Valley, rather than Sugarloaf, making it clear that town and resort were distinct and separate. They elected a new select board, with Larry Warren as first selectman, Robert A. Page and Alden Macdonald for two-year terms, and Gordon Bither and Jean Doughty for one-year terms. Rhonda Willett, Jean Luce, and Trudy Sullivan were elected to the school board. The planning board, consisting of chairman Norton Luce, Phoebe Stowell, Burnham "Bud" Ragon, and Carol Stratton, was tasked with developing a comprehensive plan. Finally, voters backed the original select board's vision of a recreation-based economy by investing $50,000 in a recreation facilities endowment fund, which was to be built up over time with annual contributions. "We decided we wouldn't spend any money from it unless we matched it [with a third-party contribution]," Warren said. "If we had

$50,000, we could turn that into $100,000 quickly. And if we played our cards right, we could turn it into $150,000. And if we had $150,000, what could we do with it? Holy mackerel, we could do whatever we wanted!"

BLAZING TRAILS

They settled on developing a Nordic ski touring center and, again drawing inspiration from Barringer's *Maine Manifest*, founded a community development corporation, the Western Mountains Corporation (later renamed Western Mountains Foundation), to do it. Barringer liked private-public entities because they could operate profit-making ventures for public benefit free of the political and bureaucratic constraints that come with government programs. The Western Mountains Corporation designed the touring center to straddle Carrabassett Valley's public lot and a leased portion of the state's public lot, effectively giving the community control over both.

The project was financed to limit the town's contribution to $50,000 drawn from the recreation facilities endowment fund. A Maine Land and Water Conservation Fund grant matched that amount, and a Farmer's Home Administration loan supplied another $50,000. Dead River Company gave the town an easement on the old narrow-gauge railroad bed. Clem Begin's Sugarloaf Construction company built the 3,800-square-foot glass-fronted building and donated the deck. Michael Gammon, who operated the Ski Rack at Valley Crossing Shopping Center, leased the rental and retail shop for an amount that covered the principal and interest on the FHA loan. Sugarloaf operations manager Hazen McMullen taught Warren, the Western Mountains Corporation president, how to operate a bulldozer, and together they cleared the old tote roads to make trails, which eventually came to total forty miles.[43]

"Right from the get-go we made money," Warren said. "The Ski Rack was happy about it. Rossignol Ski Company, who sold Nordic skis and equipment, was elated. Their director came over from France, and we

---

43. Besides Warren, the Western Mountains Corporation's first directors included Alden Macdonald, treasurer; Dutch Demshar, clerk; David Spaulding, and Gardiner Defoe. Jack Lufkin was hired as the touring center's manager.

would hold auctions and raffles to raise money. We bought a groomer from PistenBully. We added snowmaking. We built an ice rink. We started fly-fishing programs in the summer."

As Carrabassett Valley's first public/private partnership, the Touring Center expanded recreational activities beyond alpine skiing and helped stabilize the local economy. Today it's the Outdoor Center, fully owned by the town, managed by Sugarloaf, and consistently ranked among the best Nordic skiing and mountain biking facilities in the Northeast.[44]

GROWING UP

Carrabassett Valley's government had no permanent headquarters for most of its first decade. Town meetings convened variously in Valley Crossing Shopping Center, the base lodge, and the Outdoor Center. The administrative office roved with the town clerk. Joyce Demshar (then Joyce Peters), the town's third clerk in the 1970s, initially conducted town business and typeset the *Irregular* from her desk at Cole Harrison Insurance Agency in the Valley Crossing Shopping Center. When that building was dismantled and moved to the mountain in 1977, she worked all three jobs from the bar at Chateau des Tagues until the town administration found a home in the basement of Preston Jordan's newly constructed house on Carrabassett Valley Drive. In 1982, Jordan successfully pressed the select board to commit to constructing a building capable of meeting the town's long-term needs. It was built next to the fire station and continues to serve as the town office today.

As Carrabassett Valley's year-round and seasonal populations grew, so did municipal personnel and infrastructure. The town hired a fire chief, Sugarloaf Ambulance & Rescue owner Ron Morin. It purchased fire trucks and fire-fighting equipment and built two fire stations, one in the valley and one on the mountain. It took over ownership and operation of the 2,800-foot airstrip that Franklin County had acquired from Leo Tague in 1968. Although townspeople saw no need for a public school, members of the Sugarloaf Regional Ski Educational Foundation worked to broaden the racing and freestyle skiing programs it had created in 1969

---

44. Western Mountains Corporation turned management over to Sugarloaf in 1987.

by creating a school that would offer both training in competitive skiing skills and a college preparatory education. Carrabassett Valley Academy opened in the basement of Richard H. Bell Interfaith Chapel with fifteen students in 1982–1983 before moving to its permanent home in the renovated Capricorn Lodge.

All the while, town meeting voters faithfully invested in the recreation facilities endowment fund, typically around $50,000 each year. In 1982, they decided to spend some of their money to develop an eighteen-hole golf course.

Talk about a golf course had been kicking around since the early 1970s when Dead River Company unveiled ambitious but never-realized plans for a resort that involved damming the Carrabassett River to create a lake and developing links around it. A golf course also had been part of a proposed resort at Bigelow Mountain, but the project was controversial and ultimately led to the creation of the thirty-six-thousand-acre Bigelow Preserve. Now the chief champions of a golf course were Larry Warren, then both a selectman and SMC president, and Peter Webber, who, since buying the Sugarloaf Inn in 1977, had become one of the mountain's most prolific condominium developers, with more than two hundred units to his credit. A world-class golf course, they said, would expand the seasonal economy, create jobs, and support the lodging and condos that were sprouting on the mountain like mushrooms after a rainfall.

1974

Sugarloaf, Maine's largest ski resort, opened for the season Friday with manmade snow and one chairlift in operation. General Manager Harry Baxter said the area borrowed and purchased enough snow-making equipment to cover a few of its many trails. With only 5 inches of natural snow cover, the season opening was the latest in Sugarloaf's history. It also marked the first time in its 18 years that the resort was not open for Christmas vacation. —*Bangor Daily News*, January 6

Warren and Webber originally envisioned a nine-hole course on the public lot, with the Outdoor Center building as a clubhouse, but when Webber, a pilot, took the renowned golf-course developer Robert Trent Jones Jr. on an aerial tour, their vision shifted. Jones liked a 1,600-acre stretch along the river, a sizable chunk of which Webber just happened to have recently purchased from Bigelow Corporation with no specific plan in mind. Most of the rest belonged to Sugarloaf. Jones's California-based team drew up a plan detailing the locations of eighteen holes, a clubhouse, and parking. The price tag (including roads, utilities, and other infrastructure designed by the Massachusetts land-planning firm Sasaki) hovered around $3.5 million.

Once again, creative financing made the project a reality. Webber and Sugarloaf conveyed their acreage to the town of Carrabassett Valley, thus freeing the golf course from property taxes and leveraging the town's ability to issue municipal bonds. Sugarloaf kicked in $1 million, raised through the sale of limited partnerships in Village on the Green, which the resort and Peter Webber were developing together under the name Mountain Greenery. Carrabassett Valley contributed another $1 million—$250,000 from the recreation endowment fund and $750,000 from the Finance Authority of Maine. It expected to reap long-term benefits: the Village on the Green and West Mountain subdivisions would grow the tax base, and Mountain Greenery, the golf course's lease holder and operator, would repay $250,000 of the town's investment over twenty years.

1974

More than 2,000 people attended the first annual Hang-gliding Festival at Sugarloaf Mountain on Saturday and Sunday. Due to high winds, the gliding competition was called off until Sunday morning, when only three gliders were able to make the descent from the summit. There were 120 entries, which made it the largest hang-gliding contest in the east. —*Bangor Daily News*, October 10

1982

Five hundred skiers turned out for the final weekend of ski-ing, May 1 and 2. The 168-day season included skiing in seven different months (November 14 to May 2). Record attendance total an approximate 300,000 skier days (i.e. one skier skiing one day). The previous high was 240,000 skier days in 1979. —*Irregular*, May 27

Voters approved the arrangement, but it wasn't without controversy. Alden Macdonald, Warren's fellow selectman and former boss, refused to sign the golf course lease. "I didn't approve of the way it's financed," he later told the *Morning Sentinel*. "All the benefits of the golf course are going to the joint venture." In the same article, others questioned Sugarloaf's influence. Most town officials—most residents, for that matter—depended on the resort for their living. "If you go back through the years and find the facilities that the town is taking responsibility for, like the golf course, it's being done for the benefit of Sugarloaf, not the town," said Carrabassett Concerned Citizens founder Sandra Rudinsky.

But Evan Reichert, the Portland planner who worked on Carra-bassett Valley's comprehensive plan, found that town and company had developed a mutually beneficial relationship. "It would be a mistake to call them synonymous," Reichert said. "It would be correct to say they're intertwined and they cooperate. The townspeople have a real sense that they need to be independent in making decisions for the town as a whole, but in areas where they have things in common, they work together."

1984

The Lloyd Cuttler Memorial Tree was installed in Gepetto's after Lloyd clipped it off on the way down Gondy Line, turn-ing his leg into something that must have looked like the main ingredient in banana bread. —*Original Irregular*, January 9

The golf course opened on September 11, 1985. Governor Joe Brennan hit the first ball, winging it left into the woods. His second winged right, also into the trees. His third went down the center. Depending on who was analyzing the plays, they demonstrated either that the course was a fresh and exciting challenge or that Brennan was a politically astute governor who had no time to hone his game. Golf publications focused on the former, rating Sugarloaf Golf Club as one of the top courses in the nation for the skill it demands of players, not to mention its stunning views of Crocker Mountain and the Bigelow Range.

"Sugarloaf Golf Club changed the culture of Carrabassett Valley," Webber said. "Amos Winter was pivotal in developing Sugarloaf, but the golf course is right behind it in the development of the town. Before the golf course, Carrabassett Valley was a winter resort. At 4 in the afternoon, there was nothing to do except go to the bars. The golf course turned it into a four-season resort, and it gave people a reason to retire in the Sugarloaf area. They built all those houses out on West Mountain, which increased the tax base tremendously." Carrabassett Valley's total taxable value rose from $77,050,000 when the golf course opened in 1985 to $181,559,000 in 1990.

1985

The 1985 hunting season officially opens in this area when Martha Ayotte hangs up her Ayotte's Country Store Deer Hunting Contest sign. This year marks the 11th anniversary of the annual contest, which entitles all hunters who weigh in their deer at the store a chance to enter the drawing for $100, and a chance to win a $25 gift certificate for bringing in the biggest buck of the season. The contest began in 1975 as a way to keep track of what was being taken out of the area. Martha has maintained a record book with the names of the hunters who have entered the contest, the size of their deer, and where they were shot. —*Original Irregular*, November 5

The town's lease agreement with Sugarloaf has endured through the resort's ownership changes. Its mortgage payments were largely covered by the rent it collected, and Sugarloaf recouped its costs with home sales in the Snowbrook, Village on the Green, and Bigelow subdivisions, according to Dutch Demshar, who was on the select board when the course was built and was the contractor for Village on the Green. "The partnership between the town and the mountain is very unusual," Demshar said. "You'll never find it anyplace else. It's worked, and it's worked because there have been honest people in town government and honest people at Sugarloaf who realize it's a good deal for everyone."

Muckraking, Carrabassett Style

Competitive mud football, a New England tradition that attracts thousands of spectators, was played for the first time in Carrabassett Valley in 1972, the same year the town was organized.

The instigators were dump-party founder David Rolfe and selectman Parker Hall. While brainstorming additions to the valley's repertoire of oddball events, Hall described seeing some area transplants from University of Maine tossing the pigskin against seasonal-home owners in a muddy field at the end of the Carrabassett Valley airstrip. That September, two six-man teams—seasonal residents and the local Carrabassett Valley Rats—went up against each other in that same mucky field, an event billed as the first annual World Mud Bowl.

The next year, ABC's *Wide World of Sports* covered the games, and soon mud football teams were forming around New England. Rolfe founded the World Mud Football League and invited teams from Portland, Vermont, and New Hampshire to join. The league had a two-weekend season, with the finals in Carrabassett. Days before each Mud Bowl, the Rats pumped swamp water onto the 100-by-50-foot field, turning it into knee-deep muck that Hall would then rototill.

In 1981, the contest moved to Kingfield and became part of Kingfield Days in July. Now known as the Western Mountains Mud Football Challenge Cup, the two days of games are organized by longtime Rats Bob Moore and Ronk Beedy. The Mount Washington Valley Hogs, meanwhile, host the World Mud Bowl every September at Hog Coliseum in North Conway. Both contests, along with the Rats' annual auction, raise money for charity.

Interlude

MINUTES OF THE
FIRST TOWN MEETING

The meeting was called to order by Frederick W. Jones, justice of the peace, at approximately 7:30 p.m., March 15, 1972. Mr. Jones read the call to the town and the constable's return. Seven articles were discussed and decided on.

Article 1. Mr. Joseph Williamson made a motion to nominate Mr. John L. Salisbury as moderator. The motion was seconded by Mr. Preston Jordan, and no further nominations were made. It was then moved, seconded, and voted nominations cease. The vote was taken by paper ballot with Mr. Jones indicating all voters had the privilege of casting a ballot if they desired. Mr. Jones announced that all votes cast were for Mr. Salisbury and declared him elected. Mr. Frederick W. Jones, justice of the peace, then administered the oath of office to Mr. Salisbury.

Article 2. To see if the town will vote to establish a three-member board of selectmen, who will also serve as assessors, overseers of the poor, and road commissioners, to be elected for three-year terms, provided, however, that at the first election one shall be elected for a one-year term, one shall be elected for a two-year term, and one shall be elected for a three-year term. Mr. Ken Packard made a motion to accept Article 2 as written, and the motion was seconded by Mr. Ed Rogers. Mr. Salisbury asked for a show of hands, and the article was immediately passed as written. Mr. Jordan again motioned that article 6 be taken up, and it was seconded by Mr. John Rolfe. The motion was passed unanimously.

Article 6. To see what sum the town will vote to compensate the board of selectmen and the school committee. Mr. Jordan motioned that the first selectman be paid $750, the second and third selectmen be paid $500 each, and the school committee be paid $150 each. Mr. Dick Keough seconded the motion and discussion was held. Mr. David Rolfe moved that an amendment be made to the original motion that all the selectmen be paid $100, and the school committee $5 per meeting with a maximum of $50. The motion was seconded by Mr. Bruce Smith, and more debate followed. A vote by show of hands was taken on Mr. Rolfe's proposed amendment, and the motion passed with 13 in favor and 9 opposed. The moderator then called for a vote on the original motion as amended, which passed unanimously.

Article 3. To elect a board of selectmen. Nominations for a selectman to serve a three-year term were opened as Mr. Williamson nominated Mr. Jordan. Mrs. Martha Ayotte seconded the nomination. Mr. Smith was nominated by Mr. Keough but declined. Mr. Larry Warren was nominated by Mr. Rogers, and it was seconded by Mr. John Rolfe. Mr. George Willett was nominated by Mrs. Edna Judson. Mrs. Willett declined for her husband in his absence. Mrs. Ayotte was nominated by Mrs. Catherine Morrow, and it was seconded by Mrs. Judson. Mr. David Rolfe motioned that the nominations cease, and it was seconded by Mr. Richard Ayotte. The motion was passed by a show of hands. The vote was taken by paper ballot with the following results: Mr. Warren—12; Mr. Jordan—10; Mrs. Ayotte—3. The moderator indicated that no candidate had received a majority so a second vote would be necessary. It was agreed that the person receiving the lowest number of votes cast would be dropped from the list of candidates in the runoff. Mr. Jordan was elected then with 13 votes, Mr. Warren receiving 11.

Nominations for a selectman to serve a two-year term were asked for. Mr. Williamson was nominated by Mr. Jordan, and it was seconded by Mrs. Ayotte. Mr. Warren was nominated by Mr. Smith, and it was seconded by Miss Joyce Peters. Mr. Packard was nominated by Mr. Bruce Miles, and he declined. Mr. Keough motioned that nominations cease, and it was seconded by Mr. Frank Rogers. Nominations were closed, and the vote was taken by paper ballot. Mr. Warren was elected with 16 votes, Mr. Williamson receiving 9 votes.

Nominations for a selectman to serve a one-year term were opened with the nomination of Mr. Williamson by Mr. Ed Rogers. Mrs. Ayotte was nominated by Mr. Warren, Mr. Ed Rogers by Mrs. Shirley Smith, and Mr. Parker Hall by Mr. Keough. A motion to cease nominations was made by Mr. Packard and passed. The vote was taken by paper ballot with results as follows: Mr. Williamson—9; Mr. Hall—6; Mrs. Ayotte—5; and Mr. Rogers—5. A second vote was taken with Mr. Williamson receiving 10 votes, Mr. Hall 7, Mr. Rogers 5, and Mrs. Ayotte 3. Mrs. Ayotte's name was withdrawn from the list of candidates, and a third vote was taken. Mr. Hall received 14 votes, the majority; Mr. Williamson received 11; and Mr. Rogers received 1.

The moderator certified the following three selectmen elected: Mr. Preston Jordan, Mr. Larry Warren, and Mr. Parker Hall.

Article 4. To elect three members to the school committee.

Nominations were opened for the school committee by Mr. Ed Rogers' nomination of Mrs. Smith. Mrs. Rhoda Willett was nominated by Mr. Ayotte and declined. Mr. Charles Clark was nominated by Mr. Jordan, and Mrs. Elinor Clark by Miss Peters. Both Mr. and Mrs. Clark declined. Mrs. Ayotte was nominated by Mr. Steven Morrow and Mrs. Gail Jordan was nominated by Mrs. Ayotte. Mr. Ayotte motioned that nominations cease, and the motion was passed. The vote was taken by paper ballot, and the school committee chose Mrs. Smith with 9 votes, Mrs. Jordan with 9 votes, and Mrs. Ayotte with 8 votes.

Article 5. To see if the town will authorize the Board of Selectmen to appoint one person to serve as tax collector, treasurer, and clerk and to appoint all other necessary officers.

Mr. David Rolfe motioned that the article be approved as written, and it was seconded by Mr. Smith. There was no discussion. A show of hands passed the motion, and the article was accepted.

Article 7. Shall an ordinance entitled "Establishment of the Town of Carrabassett Valley Planning Board" be enacted?

Mr. David Rolfe motioned that the article be approved as written, and it was seconded by Mr. John Rolfe. No discussion was held on this article, and it was passed by a show of hands with 12 voting for and 4 voting against.

Mr. Salisbury appointed and swore as temporary clerk Miss Maralyn J. Beck.

True Copy Attest: Maralyn J. Beck
Temporary Clerk

10

Boom, Boom, Bust

SUGARLOAF GOLF CLUB'S 1985 OPENING WAS A PIVOTAL MOMENT IN Carrabassett Valley's maturation, but the town had already changed dramatically in the thirteen years since its foundation. With condo and commercial villages bourgeoning around Sugarloaf's base, for example, the town had hired Bill Gilmore to be its first code enforcement officer and building inspector. Dead River Company, meanwhile, had gotten out of the real-estate business and sold all its undeveloped Carrabassett Valley land—about twenty-four thousand acres—to the Penobscot Nation, which has since used it primarily for lumbering and allowed public recreation. A much smaller property transaction in April 1985 spoke to the town's cultural transformation. That was the foreclosure sale of the Red Stallion. Never a big moneymaker, according to Ed Rogers, the restaurant and inn had suffered as the mountain evolved into the community's social center. The Stallion's hard-partying clientele had grown up as well, and the new people buying condos were a more mature bunch than the early Sugarloafers.

The development compass had been pointed in the mountain's direction since the late 1960s. Around the same time that valley denizens began debating self-government, Sugarloaf Mountain Corporation had launched an aggressive initiative to transform the ski area into a full-fledged resort. "They decided that in order to grow, they had to build some beds," Larry Warren said. "There weren't more than 200 beds in the valley, and on busy weekends, people were driving to the mountain from hotels in Farmington, Waterville, and Lewiston."

In 1977, Larry Warren, Lloyd Cuttler and Tom Hildreth purchased the Valley Crossing Shopping Center and had it dismantled and moved to the mountain to create Village West. COURTESY OF LLOYD CUTTLER

Sugarloaf's remoteness required it to build a community nearly from scratch.
SAMUEL TRAFTON/MAINE DRONE IMAGING

SMC had formed Mountainside Real Estate, whose first task was to acquire the Sugarloaf Inn from the Pfeifles in fall 1969. With a double chairlift serving a new five-acre beginners' slope between the inn and the base lodge, guests could now step out the door, put on their skis, and be on the mountain in minutes. Mountainside created a brochure appealing to a sophisticated clientele. It included a photo of two young couples in hip après-ski togs relaxing by a metal cone fireplace. One of the men strummed a banjo. Two uncorked bottles of wine stood in the foreground. "Swinging evening life every night of the week," the caption read.

In early 1970, just a few months after buying the inn, SMC had sent a letter to season-ticket holders detailing its plans to build Mountainside Condominiums. Ownership of an individual dwelling unit within a multi-unit housing structure was a relatively new legal concept in the United States, and nothing like it existed in Maine, though a law clearing the way for condominium developments had been on the books since

1965. A precursor to the Maine Condominium Act, the Unit Ownership Act established a regulatory structure for budgets, fees, associations, and common areas. Its author was Waterville state senator—and SMC board member—Bob Marden.

Mountainside's first phase comprised twenty 900-square-foot three-bedroom units at the base of the number 4 lift. All but one of them had sold for the asking price of $19,000 within ten days of SMC's sales-pitch letter. "We didn't build anything we hadn't sold, because the corporation didn't have any money to put upfront for the whole inventory of condominiums," Warren said. "We structured it so we had construction financing that was backed by purchase-and-sale agreements and deposits. If you put $1,000 down and got a loan approved by local banks, then we built a condominium. We'd borrow the money to build the unit, close, pay off the construction loan, and give the keys to the new owner."

Prefabricated by Massachusetts-based Acorn Structures, the condos, housed in three separate buildings, went up fast and were ready for occupancy in the fall of 1970. "We didn't make any money on them, but we got the project off the ground," Warren said. "The first buyers, for the most part, were people from Maine and Massachusetts who'd been skiing at Sugarloaf since the 1950s."

The next year, Sugarloaf built and sold twenty-one units for $19,900 each. The third phase added another twenty condos, three- and four-bedroom units that sold for $24,000–$28,000.

EVERYTHING (ALMOST) IS GOING UPHILL

Sugarloaf's ambitions had rapidly shifted the town's commercial focus away from the former Jerusalem Township area to the mountain's base. In 1972, the resort built Village Center, a business and residential-condo complex. Among the first tenants was the Bag, which abandoned its digs in Valley Crossing Shopping Center. Other tenants included David Luce's photography shop, Dick and Martha Ayotte's grocery store, and Harvey Boynton's ski shop. Boynton's A-frame shop—a fixture on the mountain since 1960—was razed, bringing an end to "Boynton's Beach," the upstairs decks where skiers rendezvoused, drank beer, and soaked up the sun.[45] "Village Center gave a commercial focus to Sugarloaf after 4 o'clock," Warren said. "Before that, the parking lots emptied out, and everything was dark and dead." It was the first base village at a ski area in the East.

In 1977, the entire Valley Crossing Shopping Center was moved from Valley Crossing to the mountain, where it was named Village West. The building had to be disassembled into fourteen pieces, de-roofed to fit under power lines, transported on a convoy of flatbed trucks, and reassembled on the new site. That anyone would consider such a scheme is outlandish, so naturally Larry Warren was involved.[46] Warren had a personal interest in the building: It was home to the Truffle Hound, the fine-dining restaurant he'd started with Ted Jones and Ed Rogers in 1972. As Sugarloaf's comptroller and Carrabassett Valley's first selectman, Warren also was invested in helping the resort expand. As he explained it, other New England resorts had relatively populous communities with retail shops and lodging at their base, but Sugarloaf's remoteness required it to build a community nearly from scratch. Warren's partners in the building relocation were Tom Hildreth (director of Sugarloaf's group sales) and Lloyd Cuttler (a civil engineer and the Truffle Hound's bartender). The trio purchased the building from Dead River Company and earmarked the first and second floors for businesses, including the Truffle Hound and Cuttler's new venture, Gepetto's restaurant. Residential condos were sold on the third and fourth floors.

Flanagan's—Larry Sullivan and Joe Williamson's restaurant in the former Bag space—didn't follow the building to the mountain. Instead, Sullivan and Williamson made it into an Italian restaurant, Tufulio's, and expanded it on the shopping center's former footprint (the name is a self-deprecating reference to the two fools they considered themselves to be). With Chris Hutchins, they also built the Hotel Carrabassett, which was later converted to Valley Crossing One Condominiums.

---

45. Boynton opened his first shop on the mountain in the Sugarloaf Ski Club base lodge in 1952. He also had a Kingfield store.

46. Dutch Demshar summed up Larry Warren's approach to projects this way: "I would ask Larry, 'Why are we doing this?' Larry would always reply with the same verbatim response: 'If it was easy, someone else would have done it.'"

SELLING CONDOS LIKE POPCORN

Like many of the early Sugarloafers who built homes and commercial buildings in Carrabassett Valley, Peter Webber never planned to be a real-estate developer. Yet in less than ten years, he went from being a traveling ski salesman to builder of hundreds of condominiums, a health club, and the eighteen-hole golf course—all in Carrabassett Valley—plus the sixty-two-acre Eastward on the Ocean development in Rockport. His evolution began in 1976 with an out-of-the-blue suggestion that he and his wife, Martha, might enjoy innkeeping.

Webber's passion was skiing. As one of Amos Winter's Bigelow Boys, he'd skied Sugarloaf for the first time at age fourteen in 1949, and he'd raced in the national junior championships in Utah in 1953. He was a talented golfer, who competed in the junior golf championships at Yale in 1954, when he was taking a gap year between high school and college. After graduating from Middlebury College, where he was captain of the ski team, Webber returned to Farmington and, with his father, opened Maine's first full-line ski shop. More shops, in Waterville, Auburn, Augusta, and Carrabassett Valley, followed. In the late 1960s, his acquaintanceship with K-2 representatives led to a job as eastern sales manager for the Washington-based ski manufacturer.

It was a good fit at first, but as the Webber family grew to include three young children, Peter felt the strain of being on the road. Nevertheless, when Susan Mason of Mountainside Real Estate called him with a proposal—"Would you be interested in buying the Sugarloaf Inn?"—his gut response was "Are you crazy?" A job on the mountain was appealing, but, as Webber would explain many years later, he and Martha knew nothing about running an inn.

Several weeks after Mason's call, while sitting in Chicago's O'Hare Airport, Webber had a change of heart. He had just arrived on the red-eye from Seattle. A full day of travel lay ahead of him. "This isn't working," he realized. When he got home to Farmington, he and Martha talked it over, called Mason, and agreed to rent the inn with an option to buy.

Theirs was a sharp learning curve. "Martha and I worked our butts off," Webber said. Their first chef walked off the job on December 23,

1980

It was only a rehearsal, but a snow dance at the Penobscot reservation in Old Town was followed 24 hours later by the best skiing of the season at Maine's largest ski area. Sugarloaf Mountain is looking for an even bigger snowfall after a group of Penobscots performs its ritual dance Saturday around a bonfire outside the base lodge. Was the rehearsal responsible for the long-awaited snow? "We believe anything," said Sugarloaf spokesman Chip Cary. —*The Standard-Speaker* (Hazelton, Pennsylvania), January 25

leaving them to prepare one hundred Christmas dinners. With friends' help, they pulled it off—barely.

There were other stumbles that first year, but by the summer of 1976 the Webbers were confident enough in their innkeeping abilities to pick up their option and buy the inn and three acres for $280,000. Webber knew through his travels for K-2 that condos had become integral to ski-resort development. The formula, as Webber described it to *Down East* editor Davis Thomas, was nearly identical to that employed by Sugarloaf on the Mountainside project: a developer acquires land near the ski lifts and puts up a few model units. Additional units are then pre-sold to buyers, who consider them both retreats and investments. When not using their condos, owners turn them over to a rental agent, who is often the builder. "Thus, if all goes well, everybody is a winner," Thomas wrote. "The mountain company benefits from the creation of rental beds. The buyer gets a prestigious vacation hideaway that could turn out to be a good investment. And the developer not only reaps a profit from building and selling the units, but can charge a management fee for renting these same units to vacationers who, in turn, are excellent prospects for the sale of additional condominiums."

Webber used the formula to build Birchwood condominiums, beginning with fourteen units in 1978 (the Webbers also expanded the inn by

---

1982

On Sunday, nearly 70 firemen from 15 fire departments attended an all-day fire-fighting session at Carrabassett Valley. Two abandoned homes located just off Route 27, across from the former Bigelow Station were used for the training session. These houses were built at the turn of the century and were two of seven that originally housed families employed at the nearby Prouty and Miller mill. The houses were first filled with smoke, thereby enabling the firemen to use their air packs. Subsequently, they were burned down by the departments.
—*Irregular,* December 9

---

twenty rooms). They sold quickly. He erected ten condos the next year, then fourteen, then twenty-nine, then forty. Soon, he was "buying land like crazy." By the time Sugarloaf Golf Club was completed in 1985, his portfolio included an expanded Sugarloaf Inn, the Sugartree Club fitness center, more than one hundred Birchwood condos, forty Sugartree condos, the seventeen-home Woody Creek subdivision, twenty-three Commons townhouses, and forty condos at the former Blue Ox Lodge, which he renamed Timberwind.[47]

Only Sugarloaf/USA had built more: three hundred condos, fifty single-family homes, and the $8 million 102-room Sugarloaf Mountain Hotel and Conference Center, which had opened shortly after the golf course did. In addition, Sugarloaf operated a ski shop, ski rental shop, ski school, and nursery, and it managed several properties leased to private operators, including nine restaurants, a clothing store, three gift shops, a grocery store, and an interior furnishings store. In the works, in partnership with Webber, was Village on the Green, with about one hundred condos and thirty houses.

---

47. Albert and Milu Webber (no relation to Peter) opened the Blue Ox Lodge in 1972. It had thirty-four housekeeping units. Peter Webber converted those to condos and subsequently added six units.

Village on the Green's designers were John and Cynthia Orcutt (architect and landscape architect, respectively), who'd worked on the golf course project as employees of Sasaki. Now working for Sugarloaf, the Orcutts drew up plans for Snowbrook Village condominiums at the base of the Snubber trail and West Mountain Village above the golf course, Carrabassett Valley's highest-elevation neighborhood with a mix of townhouses and single-family houses. "We were selling condos like popcorn," Warren said.

Carrabassett Valley's tax rate, meanwhile, was $7 per $1,000 assessed valuation. The tax bill on a $100,000 property, in other words, was a mere $700. "It is no wonder 25 percent of the condos here are merely investments owned by absentee landlords, many of whom have never spent a night on Sugarloaf Mountain," Ken Becker wrote in the *Maine Sunday Telegram*. "The resident population is small, 107, according to the 1980 census. The town now lists 203 registered voters. The year-round people live off the tourist trade and the condo owners. Most of them are tied to either the mountain corporation or Webber."

The real-estate market was so brisk, in fact, that it obscured a grim reality: Sugarloaf wasn't making enough money to sustain its rapid growth. Revenues between 1975 and 1984 rose from $3 million to $10.7 million, but that growth failed to keep SMC abreast of the rising cost of its physical expansion. Sugarloaf ended the fiscal year on June 30, 1985, with a net loss of $394,000 on $11.9 million in revenues. Corporate leaders acknowledged in their annual report to stockholders that the scope of Sugarloaf's construction program "was greater than management's ability to plan, control, and coordinate." Loans of $2.5 million in 1984, $1.5 million in August 1985, and $1.1 million November 1985 were fully drawn, and a $500,000 line of credit with the Bank of Boston was fully extended. The resort was $20 million in debt.

In a press release, Warren blamed cost overruns on condo construction, a higher level of fixed expenses committed as part of Sugarloaf's expansion program, and two back-to-back warm winters. Looking back years later, Warren said, "I remember Washington's Birthday week in 1985. The temperature was 70 degrees. Water was running off the mountain, down the road. I could see our cashflow dribbling down with the rainwater. The Bank of Boston, our lead bank, was getting nervous as a cat and putting pressure on Sugarloaf and its board."

To meet the Bank of Boston's demand for more collateral, Sugarloaf's directors personally guaranteed $2.6 million in debt, but by January 1986 the resort had an operating loss of $1.2 million, nearly twice what it was the year before. In March, Sugarloaf's directors filed for protection from creditors while the company reorganized under Chapter 11 of the U.S. Bankruptcy code. A few months later, with lenders pressing for new management, Larry Warren resigned.

On September 4, 1986, the accounting firm of Peat, Marwick, Mitchell & Co. underscored just how dire Sugarloaf's financial situation was. In a report to the board of directors, the accountants wrote that "the company has incurred net losses during 1986 and 1985, and as of June 30, 1986, the company's current liabilities exceeded its current assets by $12,957,043. These factors, among others, indicate that the company may be unable to continue in existence."

Forever Winter

On August 4, 1985, a photo of fifteen-year-old Aimee Ayotte skiing in her bathing suit at Sugarloaf was carried in newspapers across the country. The thirty-five-yard-long slope was one of four mounds of snow that Stratton mill owner Adrian Brochu had covered in a reflective insulating material in April. He wanted to prove "that we can keep snow through the summer right through to fall," Brochu told ABC TV at the slope's unveiling. He called his invention Foil-Ray.

Brochu had come up with the idea the previous winter while watching snow guns shower Sugarloaf's slopes from the chairlift and lamenting the expense involved in making a product that would disappear come spring. He and his brother, Andre, partnered with Energy Saver Imports of Broomfield, Colorado, to manufacture Foil-Ray, an aluminum foil-polyethylene material similar to insulation used in building projects.

Energy Saver Imports vice president Bowen Hyma attended the August ski event. "The aluminum gives a reflectivity of the infrared rays. Instead of being absorbed by the snow, the foil bounces them off," Hyma said. "It's very, very effective. There are ski areas all over this country that are going to be very, very interested in this project."

Brochu and his team tested different methods on each of the four snow piles. The one uncovered August 4 had no protection other than the insulation. A second Foil-Ray-covered pile sat on a foot of sawdust. The third sat on sawdust and had two Foil-Ray layers. Sawdust was placed on top of the fourth insulated pile.

"The big problem in World Cup competition for the last five years in Europe is that the early season is a washout," said Nicholas Howe, a writer for *Skiing* and *Ski Racing* magazines who watched the bathing-suited skiers glide down the slope and side-step their way back to the top for another run. "The organizers spend most of their time looking for snow, and the teams travel 'round and 'round and 'round trying to find a patch here and a patch there. The cost involved in moving 15 national teams around Europe looking for snow is fantastic. The bother and hassle and trashing your skis on rocks— you wipe out your whole season's worth of equipment in the first two weeks. A thing like this, if it was developed to a science that would cover a slope, would revolutionize early-season skiing."

Nothing ever did come of Foil-Ray, though climate scientists are putting a similar idea into practice in northern Italy. Every summer since 2019, they've covered 143,500 square yards of Presena Glacier with tarpaulin in an attempt to block the sun's rays and slow the melting of snow and ice. Closer to home, faculty and students at University of Vermont are testing and refining methods of storing snow through summer with a goal of reliable late fall and early winter skiing.

Interlude

THE FLIGHT OF THE
VIRGIN ATLANTIC FLYER

At 4:12 a.m. on Thursday, July 2, 1987, two hundred people stood transfixed on Sugarloaf's summit as a black-and-silver hot-air balloon rose from the valley below. They marveled at the balloon's enormity: bigger than a twenty-one-story building. Big enough to engulf a jumbo jet. Strong enough to carry a two-decker bus.

The balloon's actual payload was rather small—a pressurized capsule, eight feet high by eight and a half feet in diameter, in which two men sat strapped to seats facing a panel of flight instruments. The captain was thirty-six-year-old English aviation and entertainment tycoon Richard Branson. The pilot was thirty-nine-year-old Swedish-born Briton Per Lindstrand, whose company, Thunder and Colt, had built the balloon, named the *Virgin Atlantic Flyer*. Their mission: make the world's first-ever hot-air-balloon crossing of the Atlantic Ocean, from Carrabassett Valley to the United Kingdom.

Balloonists had long insisted such a feat was impossible because a hot-air balloon couldn't carry enough fuel to maintain lift across the Atlantic. But the *Virgin Atlantic Flyer* was designed with a transparent outer envelope to trap the sun's warmth and heat the main balloon eighteen hours a day. Liquid-propane burners were to be used only during takeoff and to top off the hot air during hours of darkness.

Flight planners chose western Maine for the launch because of the way cold nighttime air settles in the natural bowls formed by the mountains. In those conditions, wind is often not a factor for several hours each day.

A poster commemorating the flight of the *Virgin Atlantic Flyer* hangs in WSKI-TV's office.

On a day before the launch, Richard Branson demonstrated the tight quarters he and Per Lindstrand were about to share. COURTESY OF COURTNEY KNAPP

In May, the team's technicians arrived to test launch sites near Sugarloaf, settling on Village on the Green, the luxury-home development adjacent to Sugarloaf Golf Club. On June 16, a heavy-lift airplane from London delivered the capsule to Bangor International Airport, where it was loaded on a flatbed and driven to the launchpad on Village on the Green's common. Over the next two weeks, the launch was scheduled and postponed three times as the team held out for an ideal weather pattern.

When those conditions arrived, the ground crew unrolled the balloon for the first time alongside the launchpad. There, on the afternoon before the flight, pilot and captain held an impromptu press conference at which Lindstrand described the mechanism that would release the capsule from the balloon on landing: The ring that connected the two pieces was outfitted with explosive bolts that the crew would fire when they touched down. This arrangement would prevent the balloon from dragging the capsule along the ground. Even so, Lindstrand said, "Landing is like a controlled crash. It is certain to be violent."

At midnight, the ground crew stepped inside the ginormous inflatable with propane burners to heat the air. About an hour later, the balloon lifted upright and, held in place by three large vehicles, hovered over an awed crowd. Around 3:00 a.m., spectators began boarding the chairlift to the summit.

Now, from their 4,237-foot-high perch, they *oohed* and *ahhed* as the balloon floated skyward. They didn't know what the people on the ground had just witnessed with alarm: a pair of propane tanks falling from the capsule just as it took off. But the flight team was reassuring: the *Virgin Atlantic Flyer* had more than enough remaining fuel.

All day Thursday and into the night, a strong wind drove the *Virgin Atlantic Flyer* at an average speed of one hundred miles per hour. The distance record of 907 miles, which had been set over land, was broken at 1:22 p.m., when the balloon was 104 miles east of St. John's, Newfoundland, at an altitude of 27,900 feet.

The *Flyer* reached the Irish coast around 2:00 p.m. EDT on Friday. After descending from twenty-seven thousand feet, the capsule scraped through a field and bashed into a stone wall near Limavady, losing two fuel tanks. Regaining altitude, the now badly damaged *Flyer* proceeded east, back over the ocean. When Lindstrand attempted to land on Rathlin Island, the explosive bolts failed to release the balloon. It dragged and bounced the gondola over the water's surface at high speed before it lifted yet again. Fearing for his life, Lindstrand threw himself off the gondola's roof. Still inside, Branson put on an oxygen mask and prepared to parachute, but instead he flew the balloon down. The capsule was sixty feet above the water when Branson jumped. He was quickly picked up by a helicopter. Lindstrand, without a life vest, spent more than two hours swimming against strong current in cold water before some kids in a rubber dinghy picked him up, a Royal Navy helicopter flying overhead. Both men were taken to the hospital for observation.

It took a while for news of the rescue to reach Sugarloaf. At first, all anyone knew was that the men had bailed out over the Irish Sea. Some of the fifty or so people gathered at project headquarters in the Sugarloaf Mountain Hotel feared the worst. "When it was confirmed that the pair was on dry land, and the *Virgin Atlantic Flyer* was down, corks popped, but there were no shouts of glee," Jack McKee reported in the *Lewiston Daily Sun*. "Persons who had been operating with little or no sleep for the past 50 to 55 hours were much too relieved and too exhausted to engage in frivolous celebration. Their concern was still for the two men they sent aloft from Sugarloaf at 4:12 a.m. Thursday. 'Thank God they are okay' was the near prayerful comment from all."

The Paris-based International Aeronautics Federation determined that the Virgin Atlantic Flyer's *2,900-mile flight set a world distance record. Branson and Linstrand also hold the current distance record in that ballooning category: 6,700 miles set on January 1991 with the* Virgin Pacific Flyer.

11

Tightening the Bond

SUGARLOAF'S FINANCIAL TROUBLES WERE OF GRAVE CONCERN TO CAR-
rabassett Valley residents and property owners. The ski area employed 650
people, and its properties accounted for 70 percent of the town's total
assessed value. The town owed its existence and economic welfare to the
mountain. That's why voters at a special town meeting convened a few
months after SMC's bankruptcy filing approved a four-year moratorium
on the resort's lease payments on the golf course and agreed to spend
$95,000 to pay for its cost overruns. That was just the beginning. Over
the next few years, Carrabassett Valley would come to Sugarloaf's aid two
more times before the resort's finances stabilized.

COURTESY OF JAMIE WALTER

When Sugarloaf filed for reorganization bankruptcy, mortgage rates were high, and the demand for second homes had gone cold. Sugarloaf also had aggressive new competition. Eighty miles south at Sunday River in Newry, Les Otten was rapidly transforming the once-modest ski area into one of the biggest in the East, adding trails and lifts and an extensive snowmaking operation. As part of Sugarloaf's reorganization plan, SMC chairman King Cummings temporarily assumed the role of chief executive officer and assembled a new management team. Cummings's nephew, Warren Cook, left his position as CEO of a New Hampshire textile firm and replaced Larry Warren as president of both SMC and Mountainside. Cummings and Cook shifted the resort's focus away from real-estate development to improving the skiing experience.

The new direction became evident almost immediately. The bankruptcy court approved Sugarloaf's plan to raise money to expand snowmaking by selling the incomplete Snowbrook and Bigelow condominium projects for $2 million. The buyer, Portland-based Dartmouth Company, replaced Mountainside as the exclusive brokerage office for properties at Sugarloaf/USA. The court simultaneously approved SMC's request to obtain a $2.5 million working capital loan for operations. "These were key to refloating the company and having a more successful operation," Cook explained decades later.

Spirits rose in the winter of 1986–1987, as the first new snowmaking machines blasted away and added to the abundant natural snow. Then more help arrived in the form of a Merrill Bank loan of $4 million, made all the sweeter by the fact that the Finance Authority of Maine, recognizing Sugarloaf's significant impact on the northern Franklin County economy, had insured more than half of it.

Cummings and Cook raised another $7 million in equity from a new group of stockholders. With their investments, these twenty individuals came to own 96 percent of SMC. Cummings was the biggest shareholder with 25 percent ownership.

When Sugarloaf emerged from bankruptcy protection in the summer of 1987, it had issued $12 million in checks to banks and secured creditors, with another $1.4 million placed into a fund to pay unsecured creditors 50 percent of the amount they were owed. In an interview with

Sunrise over the Bill Munzer Recreational Bridge at the northwest end of Sugar-loaf Regional Airport. COURTESY OF DAVID COTA

the *Lewiston Daily Sun*, King Cummings acknowledged that, in the years leading up to the bankruptcy filing, many people in Carrabassett Valley and surrounding towns had voiced concerns that Sugarloaf was neglecting mountain improvements as it pursued real-estate development. "In thinking through the problems of Sugarloaf, the key, most important one was the lack of communication with the communities around Sugarloaf and the skiers," Cummings said. "My hope—and we've started with the chamber of commerce and the communities—is that we build on the vital importance of all of us working together for the future."

RECOVERY

By the summer 1988, Sugarloaf had invested $8 million in modernizing lifts, trails, grooming, and the base lodge. Snowmaking had been increased by 400 percent, and the new East Mountain and King Pine Bowl added 440 acres of new skiing terrain. Satisfied that the mountain's finances and priorities were moving in the right direction, Cummings stepped down from the chairman's seat and became vice chair. Peter Webber was elevated from vice chair to chairman.

Sugarloaf still had a long way to go to become profitable, however, so its twenty major shareholders—several of whom were not interested in a long-term investment—took note of a new phenomenon: Japanese companies were buying struggling U.S. ski resorts. "King died in 1989, so we lost one of the key leaders. That was unsettling for a lot of people," Cook recalled. "My investor group got the idea that they should sell to the Japanese. We put together a package in 1990, but we were late in the game. I told the investors we wouldn't be getting the high price that the Japanese had paid at other resorts. And sure enough, when we did get an offer, it didn't meet the investors' expectations."

Cook took another tack: He put together a team of five investors who proposed buying Sugarloaf Mountain Corporation for $2.7 million in cash and $750,000 in loan guarantees.[48] The offer, which made Cook majority owner and CEO, was approved by stockholders in June 1992. Key to its success, Cook said, was Carrabassett Valley voters' willingness to loan Sugarloaf money, which they did twice in less than a year, spurred on, perhaps, by Larry Warren's recent report on the "devastating" impact of Ascutney Ski Area's closure on the town of Ascutney, Vermont.

The first loan was relatively small—$300,000 for snowmaking equipment—and stirred little controversy. Voters at a June special town meeting agreed to take the money from the recreation facilities endowment fund, so it had no impact on taxes.

In September, Cook went back to the selectmen to request a $5.5 million loan for capital improvements, including the 6,655-foot high-speed chairlift now known as the SuperQuad and forty-five acres of new and widened trails. A town study committee, whose members included Larry Warren, town manager Bill Gilmore, accountant Alden Macdonald, and lawyer Bruce Coggeshell, chose instead to focus on helping SMC reduce its $9.3 million debt.

---

48. The other investors were William E. Haggett, former head of Bath Iron Works and president of Saint John Shipbuilding in New Brunswick; Joe O'Donnell of Boston Concession Group, which ran Sugarloaf's concessionaires; James M. Seed, a Providence, Rhode Island, real-estate executive; and Jordan Lumber of Kingfield.

The committee recognized that Sugarloaf's financial troubles hadn't happened in a vacuum. During the 1980s, residential and commercial real-estate markets boomed throughout the Northeast and then turned to bust as the economy weakened. With an oversupply of newly completed projects on the market, real-estate prices had fallen and loan defaults had risen, leading to the failure of several banks. "The present status of the banking industry in New England has reduced the number of potential ski area first-mortgage lenders to one," the committee reported. "The market for ski area sales has all but been eliminated due to the non-availability of financing and the weak operational performance of the industry in the northeastern United States. These conditions do not present an encouraging prognosis for the town in the event of another financial collapse of Sugarloaf Mountain Corporation."

At the committee's request, SMC negotiated with its principal lender the discharge of its $6.7 million loan at a $1.7 million discount. The committee then crafted a complex, two-pronged proposal that was projected to reduce Sugarloaf's debt by $4.9 million with no subsidy from the town.

First, the town would form a sanitary district, managed independently of the town government, to issue $3.4 million in revenue bonds and use the proceeds to purchase Sugartech, the mountain's sewage facilities. All new construction would be required to tie into the system, and the bonds would pay for themselves through user and connection fees.

1994

The governors of Maine and New Hampshire met on the slopes of Sugarloaf/USA Friday for the third annual New England Governors Ski Challenge, with Maine's chief executive, John McKernan, and his ski team gliding to victory. Vermont Governor Howard Dean was unable to attend the event due to the snowstorm. The annual race promotes winter tourism and the importance of the ski industry on Maine's and New England's economies. —*Irregular*, January 19

1994

A piece of history went up in flames last Thursday as the Avalanche Control building was intentionally burned to give way to the new chairlift on Sugarloaf. Sometime around 1963, an employee of Bath Iron Works, George Carey, owned a camp on Route 27. When he became seriously involved with the construction of the gondola, he had his building moved to Sugarloaf, where it became known as Avalanche Control and was used as headquarters for the snowmakers. —*Irregular*, August 3

Second, the town would sell $3.7 million in general obligation bonds and loan the proceeds to SMC, which would pay the entire debt service on the bonds. SMC was required to secure a $2 million working capital line of credit, and the town and lender would share first mortgage on SMC's assets. SMC also was to ask the Finance Authority of Maine, which had guaranteed its line of credit under its principal lender, to continue that guarantee under the new arrangement.

Opponents, who didn't think the town should invest in private industry regardless of the consequences of a Sugarloaf financial failure, were surprisingly few. Voters at the March 1993 annual town meeting passed the plan 74–4. Soon after, selectmen created a loan administration committee to oversee the agreement, thus avoiding public discussions of sensitive financial information that might have been required under the freedom-of-information law if selectmen were the overseers.[49]

The strategy paid off quickly. By December, SMC had reduced its debt to less than $4.5 million. In January, S-K-I Ltd., the owner of Killington Ski Area and Mount Snow in Vermont, purchased 51 percent of the controlling interest in Sugarloaf, infusing $4.5 million into the company

---

49. The loan administration committee members were nonresident taxpayers with financial expertise: Ron Smith, the president of Cushnoc Bank and Trust of Augusta and former lending officer for Key Bank of Maine; Bill Canaan, former president of Casco Northern Bank and former senior lending officer for Fleet Bank of Maine; and Lin Morrison, president of the Bank of Ipswich in Massachusetts.

to pay for a five-year multi-million-dollar expansion of trails, snowmaking systems, and chair lifts, including the SuperQuad, capable of whisking three thousand skiers an hour up the mountain. It's unlikely either would have happened had Carrabassett Valley and Sugarloaf not crafted their creative debt-restructuring program—a plan for which they knew of no precedent. "It's quite unusual for a town to do this," said Bill Gilmore, who succeeded Preston Jordan as town manager in 1989 and served in that post until 2001. "Most towns have a variety of industries within their borders that pay taxes. To go out on a limb and ask taxpayers to float that kind of money that needs to be paid back wouldn't be fair in most places. But Sugarloaf was the one horse that generated revenue in Carrabassett Valley: No mountain, no skiers. No skiers, no home sales. No home sales, no tax money. Looking at what was on the mountain then and what is on the mountain now, the town would have been stupid not to do it."

H. King Cummings:
The Man Who Saved Sugarloaf

H. King Cummings earned statewide recognition for leading Sugarloaf out of bankruptcy, but his influence on the success of the resort and surrounding community went well beyond that. "Next to Amos Winter, King was the single person most responsible for the emergence of Sugarloaf as a major player in the world of skiing," John Christie writes in *The Story of Sugarloaf*. "In its worst of times, King stepped up and nearly single-handedly engineered its emergence from bankruptcy."

Born in Old Town in 1917, Cummings grew up in Skowhegan, where his brother, Willard W. Cummings, was one of the founders of the Skowhegan School of Painting and Sculpture. Cummings, an MIT grad, succeeded his father as president of Guilford Industries in 1950 and immediately proceeded to modernize the textile manufacturer with state-of-the-art machinery and enlarged capacity.

Cummings and his family were among Sugarloaf's earliest skiers and earliest ski-era camp owners. He was a charter member of Sugarloaf Mountain Corporation's board of directors and, from the start, the mountain's largest stockholder. He was part of the team that

King Cummings, who guided Sugarloaf through bankruptcy organization, had a profound influence on the resort and community. Here he's pictured with other founders of Carrabassett Valley Academy signing the school's first headmaster, Bruce Colon. Clockwise from top left are Art Currier, Cummings, Robert Boylestad, Colon, Jean Luce, and Ginny Bousum.
COURTESY OF CARRABASSETT VALLEY ACADEMY

hammered out an agreement with Scott Paper to purchase Sugarloaf Mountain in 1959 and Burnt Mountain in 1972. He was a key player in the founding of Carrabassett Valley Academy, as well as the Maine Community Foundation, which spearheads local improvement projects statewide, and the Western Mountains Alliance, which promotes sustainable development.

He was sixty-nine when he became Sugarloaf's board chairman and chief executive officer and assembled the team that guided the company through reorganization. Among those he brought in to help him was his nephew, Warren Cook, who became Sugarloaf Mountain Corporation president. After Sugarloaf emerged from bankruptcy, King and Peter Webber switched board positions, with King stepping down to vice chair and Webber rising to chair. Cook took over as SMC's CEO; a few years later, he became the mountain's majority owner.

Cummings was candid and transparent during Sugarloaf's reorganization. "We found him to be right up-front," Lewiston *Sun-Journal* sports reporter Dave Irons wrote in a tribute to Cummings following his death in March 1989. "He laid everything right on the table, sharing responsibility for the problems and not passing blame to someone else. He was looking forward, not back. There was a job to do, and he was going to get it done."

Interlude

STRANDED—MONSTER STORMS PROVE THE VALLEY'S METTLE

Blizzards, spring floods, and hurricanes are often sudden and severe in Carrabassett Valley. Here are some of the most significant events of the ski era.

THE "100-HOUR STORM" OF 1969

In late February 1969, a powerful storm stalled off the New England coastline for three and a half days, paralyzing the region. Ranked an extreme Category 5 on the Regional Snowfall Index, the northeaster is remembered as the "100-Hour Snowstorm."

It caught nearly everyone off-guard. The National Weather Bureau had predicted two to four inches of snow, but by nightfall on the first day, February 24, more than a foot had already fallen in some Maine towns. The wind whipped up six-foot-high drifts that plows couldn't move. Drivers abandoned their cars and sought shelter in police barracks.

It was too much snow too fast, even for the ski areas. By the storm's third day, February 26, Sugarloaf closed because its lifts were buried in drifts. "We want it to stop," general manager Harry Baxter told the *Bangor Daily News*.

Stranded hotel guests and their hosts made the best of being snowed in. At Chateau des Tagues, Leo Tague led singalongs and held contests to see who could wade the farthest in the snow. Guests scaled snowbanks to step onto the Chateau's roof and then slid down into the fluff. At the Capricorn Lodge, Charlie Clark reported that guests were in high spirits. And Don and Maryann Pfeifle said they and the kids were keeping everyone well fed and happy at the Sugarloaf Inn.

As the storm petered out on February 27, Jerusalem and Sugarloaf townships were sitting under sixty-seven inches of snow, and Route 27 was closed. People snowshoed to Valley Crossing Shopping Center to pass the time in checkers and cribbage tournaments. The next day, a state highway department snowblower truck from Aroostook County arrived to clear Route 27. Two dozen people stood on the snowbanks in the Capricorn's parking lot to watch the machine's giant auger cut through the drifts and shoot snow nearly to the river.

Side roads remained impassable for days. Fotter's Store in Eustis delivered groceries to the Capricorn, where locals loaded them onto toboggans and skis. When a logging company bulldozer opened the road to the Red Stallion, chef Dick Bixby was relieved: his cupboard was down to one bag of dog food. Governor Ken Curtis invoked an emergency provision of Maine's blue laws and authorized grocery stores to open on the Sunday after the storm.

Digging out the Harvey Boynton Ski Shop at Sugarloaf after the "100-Hour Storm" of 1969. COURTESY OF SUGARLOAF SKI CLUB

Plow crews worked extra hard that winter. The "100-Hour Snow-storm" was bracketed by two other big storms—one a powerful northeaster on February 8–10 that dumped twenty-two inches in the Longfellow Mountains region, the other an early March howler that swirled snow into big drifts and disrupted town-meeting schedules across the state. By the time the 1968–1969 ski season was over, Sugarloaf had received 347 inches of snow, surpassing the previous 1958 record by 23 inches and the mountain's average annual snowfall by 150 inches. The ski season ran 190 days that winter, from November 9 to May 11, a remarkable stretch in the days before snowmaking (Sugarloaf manufactured snow for the first time in 1973–1974). When it was over, valley denizens commemorated their resilience with bumper stickers reading, "I survived the winter of '69."

THE FLOOD OF 1987

One of the worst natural disasters in western Maine mountain weather history occurred March 30–April 1, 1987, when a storm poured five to eight inches of rain atop half a foot or more of heavy melting snow. The Kennebec River and its tributaries were the most severely impacted, the National Weather Service reported.

In Carrabassett Valley, floodwaters washed out the Route 27 S-curves, and several homes were damaged. Some people were without power for days. Ted and Kitty Jones were stranded when the flood swept away the bridge that connects their property on the east side of the river to Route 27. Water began splashing over the bridge on the afternoon of March 30. By evening, the river was rushing past two sides of the Joneses' house, and their horses were standing in ten inches of water in the barn. The next morning, they awoke to find their bridge was gone. "After we became accustomed to it, it was fun," Ted told the *Irregular*. Friends built a footbridge wide enough for Kitty's rider mower and wagon to cross with groceries and grain for the horses. "Everybody here pulls together really nicely," Ted said.

Lynn and David Chase's home at Packard's Pool sustained serious damage. Floodwaters knocked out a basement wall and filled the space to the ceiling. In the aftermath, the Chases removed forty trash cans of silt and sand from their driveway and lawn.

Statewide, losses from the flooding were estimated at $100 million. Fourteen of the state's sixteen counties were declared federal disaster areas, and 215 homes were destroyed.

TROPICAL STORM IRENE

Irene bulldozed her way through Maine on August 28, 2011, snapping limbs, felling trees, and downing power lines. The tropical storm, which had peaked in the Caribbean as a Category 3 hurricane, created disruptions throughout most of the state, but it was brutal to western Maine, especially Carrabassett Valley, which was drenched in 8.5 inches of rain.

Overflowing Carrabassett River tributaries wiped out two Route 27 bridges within minutes of each other—one just south of the Sugarloaf Access Road, the other just north of it. Canadian truck driver Yannick Livernoche was between the two bridges when they collapsed in the late afternoon at the height of the storm. Livernoche, who was headed north with a load of lime, had just crossed the second bridge when floodwaters on the road forced him to stop. No sooner had he backed over the bridge than it sank into the South Branch of the Carrabassett River. Livernoche turned his eighteen-wheeler around and drove a few hundred feet south only to find that the first bridge had crumbled into Brackett Brook. Livernoche got a ride home to Quebec a few days later, but his truck stayed put for weeks. Stranded overnight at Sugarloaf were about one hundred employees and guests, who had no way to drive out of the resort.

Irene also collapsed the bridge connecting Campbell Field to the Narrow Gauge Pathway, severely eroded the northbound lane of the Route 27 S-curves, and damaged two golf-cart bridges at Sugarloaf Golf Club. Ted and Kitty Jones once again found themselves marooned after their bridge was swept away. When Governor Paul LePage visited Carrabassett on a helicopter tour the morning after the storm, he pronounced the damage the worst he'd seen.

Road workers hastily opened a route to and from Sugarloaf via Brackett Brook Road and Bridge Street, south of the washouts. Sugarloaf employees and visitors arriving from the north had to park their cars and use a temporary footbridge. Anyone trying to get north of Sugarloaf followed a detour from Kingfield through Phillips, Rangeley, and Stratton. The resort remained in full operation: mountain bikers hit the trails, sightseers rode the lifts, and zip-line riders flew over Gondi Brook.

Hired by the state, the Woolwich firm of Reed & Reed worked through the Labor Day weekend to install two temporary bridges and reopened Route 27 on September 6. The company went on to complete the permanent spans just in time for ski-season opening day. "We had a target date of November 18," Maine Department of Transportation spokesman Ted Talbot told the *Sun-Journal*, "and we made it."

12

Building on Our Strength

RESCUING SUGARLOAF SOLIDIFIED CARRABASSETT VALLEY'S REPUTA-
tion as an innovative collaborator. So it was that the trustees of Carrabassett Valley Academy approached the board of selectmen in March 2000
with a proposal: Would the town be interested in partnering with the
school to build the most advanced gym in the state?

The academy, then in its seventeenth year, had produced nineteen
national champions, six Olympians, and five NCAA All-Americans.

CVA students train at the Anti-Gravity Complex, which is jointly owned by the
town and school. COURTESY OF CARRABASSETT VALLEY ACADEMY

Headmaster John Ritzo and the school's trustees believed CVA could turn out even more winning athletes if it had an all-season facility with "anti-gravity" equipment like trampolines to teach air awareness. They'd recently launched a fundraising campaign, which was bolstered by Sugarloaf's donation of a six-acre building site.

Shared ownerships of recreation facilities among municipalities and private schools are rare, but then again, so are debt-restructuring partnerships between towns and ski resorts. And this was a safe bet: As Ritzo put it, each owner would get a state-of-the-art fitness center for half price. Town and school would split operating costs proportionately based on each partner's use of the facility.

The various town committees that took up the proposal focused less on whether to accept it and more on what should be included in a recreation center that townspeople would support. Locals' interest was twofold, explained Jean Luce, who has been both a Carrabassett school committee member and a CVA trustee. First, residents and property owners would be able to use the facility whenever CVA students weren't training. Second, Carrabassett youngsters enrolled at CVA were among those who would benefit from the high-level instruction that academy would be able to offer.

Tom Cromwell, who took this photo, rides the valley's trails every day year-round. Cyclists consult his Instagram for trail conditions. COURTESY OF TOM CROMWELL

Riding the Narrow Gauge Pathway. COURTESY OF JAMIE WALTER

Just three months after CVA made its initial proposal, town meeting voters approved a twenty-thousand-square-foot gym, replete with skate park, climbing wall, trampolines, multi-sport court, and weight-lifting and aerobics equipment. The town's share, $600,000, came from the recreation facilities endowment fund—the nest egg they'd been growing diligently since 1975 and had used to build the touring center and the golf course, among many other things. Named the Anti-Gravity Complex, the gym opened in 2001.

Thus the people of Carrabassett Valley began the new century with yet another creative investment in their vision of an outdoor adventurer's idyll. Over the next several years, they made more. In 2003, they leveraged a $600,000 state grant to transform a sublime six-mile riverside stretch of the old rail line into the multi-use Narrow Gauge Pathway; the town's portion, $150,000, again came from the recreation fund. They built a $1 million, 5,500-square-foot golf-course clubhouse, with financing provided by an amended golf course lease with Sugarloaf Mountain Corporation; it opened in 2005. The only project that had a noticeable impact on homeowners' annual tax bills—a $48 increase on average—was the

$1.2 million Outdoor Center expansion in 2007. As longtime selectman Bob Luce put it, the bigger, cozier lodge, National Hockey League–size skating rink, and new trails would pay back the investment by attracting more visitors and second-home owners.

Private recreation-oriented businesses, institutions, and organizations expanded as well, and new ones formed: CVA built a campus and, with Sugarloaf and the Sugarloaf Ski Club, the Bill & Joan Alfond Competition Center (the town contributed $100,000 to the project). Maine Huts & Trails (MH&T), Larry Warren's creation, chose Carrabassett for the location of its first wilderness hut—Poplar Falls, which opened in 2008—and its fourth—Stratton Brook, which opened in 2012. Sugarloaf spent millions of dollars to expand snowmaking and develop new terrain. Three clubs—the Carrabassett Valley ATV Club, the Carrabassett Valley Outdoor Association, and the Carrabassett Region chapter of the New England Mountain Biking Association (CR-NEMBA)—formed.

New construction of second homes was perhaps the most visible indicator of how far the town had come economically and culturally. In an October 2003 letter to the *Irregular*, Sugarloaf Ambulance & Rescue director Ron Morin wrote of biking past a newly cleared lot at Carriage and Huston Brook roads on his way to the Narrow Gauge Pathway. "The Red Stallion is gone!" he wrote. "Another era has passed." The lot's owner, Ron Allen, had razed the former ski-bum haunt to make way for an eight-home subdivision.

Allen's project was minor in the overall picture of Carrabassett development activity that year: thirty-five single-family homes and thirty-eight condo units were built, and the value of the town's taxable property rose by $32 million. That pace was typical, even modest, for the period—in 2005, for example, Sugarloaf broke ground on five residential projects, which, when fully developed, would comprise 222 single-family, duplex, and condo dwellings: West Mountain, Fall-Line, Castle Creek, the Timbers, and North Ridge. New-house starts plummeted during the Great Recession, which began in late 2007, but by 2014 Carrabassett Valley's housing stock was growing at a good clip, and with the COVID-19 pandemic real-estate boom in the early 2020s, it resumed its former frenetic pace.

Riders in the Sugarloaf Mountain Bike Festival, which is organized by Sugarloaf, Maine Huts & Trails, and Carrabassett Region NEMBA. COURTESY OF JAMIE WALTER

YEEEEW! MOUNTAIN BIKING TAKES HOLD

Those in the latest wave of Carrabassett home buyers tell real-estate brokers they're interested in the alpine and cross-country ski trails, the golf
course, and something relatively new—mountain-biking trails. Between
2014 and 2022, the town, Sugarloaf, MH&T, and CR-NEMBA together
invested more than $700,000 and thousands of volunteer hours in building
and improving an eighty-mile network of bike trails. While there's been
no formal study of mountain biking's economic impact, there's plenty of
anecdotal evidence. Restaurants that once closed for the summer are now
operating year-round, for example, and home sales are up. "We hear from
a lot of people who say they've been thinking about buying a place in the
area for years, and now they can truly justify it because the mountain-bike
system is so big," said Sam Punderson of Mountainside Real Estate.

A small fraternity of bicyclists had been off-roading and making their
own trails in Carrabassett Valley as early as the mid-1980s, but the area
remained under the radar as a mountain-biking destination until 1992,
when Sugarloaf/USA hosted its first Widowmaker Mountain Bike Challenge Weekend, a National Off-Road Bicycle Association (NORBA)
championship-series event. The six-mile romp through the forest drew
125 competitors and a lot of press (the weekend also included dual slalom and lift-serviced downhill races). The winner was a hometown boy:

2006

Boots crunched in the snow as people shifted their weight, lean-
ing in, trying to see. A cheer was rising, then falling, then rising
again: "We want Seth! We want Seth!" It was Seth Wescott Day in
the state of Maine, and on Saturday more than 3,000 people were
standing around the Base Lodge at Sugarloaf/USA, to welcome
him home. The 29-year-old Olympic gold medalist made history
February 16 by becoming the first person ever to win gold in the
sport of snowboard cross. —*Lewiston Sun-Journal,* February 26

---

twenty-two-year-old Peter Webber Jr., who'd started off-road biking while a student at CVA and had become one of the country's top racers.

For the next few years, the Widowmaker Challenge was one of New England's biggest mountain-bike races, peaking at over one thousand racers before it morphed into a smaller event with American Skiing Company's acquisition of Sugarloaf in 1996. ASC focused primarily on downhill skiing and the golf course. It welcomed recreational bikers on most of the Outdoor Center's Nordic trails—for free—but they didn't draw anywhere near the large numbers of bikers who were flocking to Acadia National Park and New Hampshire's White Mountains. *Maine Sunday Telegram* outdoor writer Deirdre Fleming remarked on the phenomenon after riding through the Carrabassett woods in solitude in 2004. "The sport never took off in the western mountains as some thought it would," she wrote, speculating that "the heyday for real mountain-bike riding may have passed."

Some riders, like Dave Hughes, believed the opposite was true: Carrabassett Valley's mountain-biking peak lay in the future—if the town,

The annual Carrabassett Valley Backcountry Cycle Challenge attracts several hundred competitors with 25K, 50K, and 100K races. COURTESY OF BRAD AND BETH HERDER

Sugarloaf, and MH&T were willing to do more than accommodate cyclists on trails built for winter sports. Hughes took town manager (and avid mountain biker) Dave Cota and MH&T executive director Dave Herring to Kingdom Trails in Vermont so they could see the potential of a trail system designed for mountain bikes. In 2009, "the three Daves" successfully lobbied the town to fund a study assessing the viability of designing, constructing, and managing a system of trails specifically for bikes. The study was conducted by none other than Peter Webber Jr., then a trail specialist at the Colorado-based International Mountain Bike Association (IMBA) and the author of two seminal books on trail development. Webber drew up a plan that focused on upgrading the Outdoor Center's cross-country ski routes. The following year, the town contracted with Hardy Avery of Vermont-based Sustainable Trailworks to develop a three-year $106,000 trail build-out plan and hired Josh Tauses, one of the early rogue trail builders, to oversee the work (today, Tauses is Carrabassett Valley's full-time trail boss).

Local cyclists acted on another Webber recommendation: the creation of a club for trail stewardship and advocacy. They formed CR-NEMBA and organized volunteers to assist Tauses and his crew. Working alongside them were teams from MH&T. The two nonprofits' efforts attracted significant financial gifts from companies like L.L. Bean and organizations like IMBA.

2009

Paul Schipper, an avid skier who obsessively hit the slopes every day of the season for 24 years, has died. He was 85. Schipper was a legendary figure at Sugarloaf, where he and his wife owned Lumberjack Lodge. Between 1980 and January 2005, he skied 3,903 consecutive days at the mountain. Schipper once put off removing a cancerous kidney to keep his streak alive. A trail at Sugarloaf—Schipper's Streak—is named in his honor.
—Associated Press, February 17

2010

Stories are emerging of what it was like to be on the Spillway
East chairlift at Sugarloaf Mountain resort in Maine when the
cable derailed December 28—sending several chairs falling
20 or 30 feet to the ground, injuring at least eight people and
stranding about 150 others for up to a couple hours. On ABC's
Good Morning America, a young skier named Rebecca London
said, "I could feel myself falling and see the chair in front of me
falling. I didn't even realize what had happened until I was on
the ground." About two feet of fresh snow helped cushion her
landing. London wasn't hurt. —NPR, December 29

In 2014, the town, MH&T, CR-NEMBA, and Sugarloaf formalized
their collaboration as Carrabassett Valley Trails, whose work is under-
pinned by a memorandum of understanding that acknowledges their
common interests and establishes a structure for coordinating their efforts
to create mountain-biking opportunities for people of all ages and abilities. The organization's biggest fundraiser, the annual Carrabassett Valley
Backcountry Cycle Challenge, attracts several hundred competitors with
25K, 50K, and 100K races (the latter is part of the National Ultra Endurance Mountain Bike Race Series). "We're working together to develop
a mountain-bike trail system of exceptional quality, sustainability, and
diversity for enjoyment by our residents, property owners, and riders who
travel to our area," Cota said.

Today, no one would suggest that mountain biking has reached its
peak in Carrabassett Valley; rather, it's still pedaling toward it. The trail
network has grown by two to three miles a year, spreading over land
owned by the town, the state, Sugarloaf, Weyerhaeuser, and the Penobscot Nation (the Nation's land remains closed to public recreation as of
this writing). Each summer, thousands of competitive riders come to
Carrabassett Valley for events like the Carrabassett Backcountry Cycle
Challenge (part of the National Ultra Endurance Mountain Bike Race

A young rider in the 2022 Carrabassett Valley Backcountry Cycle Challenge.
COURTESY OF BRAD AND BETH HERDER

Series), the Eastern States Cup, NEMBAFest, and the Enduro World Series. Current projects include the Josh Tauses–designed fifteen-mile Stoney Brook Trails project in the state Crocker Mountain Conservation Area. Likewise, Sugarloaf has hired champion mountain-bike racer Adam Craig to guide the development of a lift-accessed mountain-bike park and build a portfolio of enduro and downhill events.

Interlude

CLEM AND ROLANDE BEGIN—
UP BY THE BOOTSTRAPS

Their names are everywhere: the Begin Family Community Room at Carrabassett Valley Public Library, Clem's Climbing Wall at the Anti-Gravity Complex, the Begin Family Room at Richard H. Bell Interfaith Chapel, and Begin's Way, which winds through the Carrabassett Valley Academy campus. Together, those dedicated places represent just a fraction of Clem and Rolande Begin's generosity to their community.

Clem and Rolande Begin hold the sign for the street named in their honor on the CVA campus. COURTESY OF DAVID COTA

French-speaking Quebec dairy farmers who came to Jerusalem Township in search of off-season jobs in 1961, the Begins soon impressed locals with their work ethic. Embraced in particular by their first employer, Leo Tague, they ended up settling in town and built a successful construction business. They've been magnanimous community members, making significant contributions to several institutions and recreation projects. "Giving back to this community and our friends is very important to us, and being able to share our good fortune with you gives us tremendous pride and satisfaction," Clem said in 2010, when he and Rolande announced gifts totaling $1.75 million to four organizations. "This place and the people who live here have given us so much to be thankful for: work, opportunities, education, and caring friends."

Childhood sweethearts, the Begins grew up on their families' farms in St. Ludger, Quebec, about fourteen miles north of Lac-Mégantic. Clem was the oldest of ten children; Rolande was one of eleven children. To ease his parents' financial burdens, Clem left home at age fifteen to work at a lumber camp in James Bay. "I started in the woods, but my first time, I said, 'I'm outta here,'" he remembered. "There were some kids working in the kitchen, and I told one of them, 'Anytime you guys want to take a day off, I'll replace you.' We had 250 men, a pretty big camp. We made all the food, rang the bell, and got out of the way because the men came in all at once."

Eager to get out of the wilderness, he took a construction job in Montreal. At nineteen, he opened a restaurant there. Every two weeks, he drove two hundred miles east to St. Ludger to spend time with Rolande, a routine that quickly wore thin. The couple married, and—after a short stint in Ontario, where Clem was again chopping trees—they bought a farm in St. Ludger and maintained a herd of sixty dairy cows.

In the winter of 1961, Clem and his brother John Paul came south to Eustis to cut wood, but it was hard going in the deep snow, so Clem inquired about a job as a cook at Roger's Motel and Restaurant (now the White Wolf Inn). Owner Roger Lavigne sent him to Leo Tague, who had recently opened Chateau des Tagues. Tague hired Clem as his chef. Soon after, Rolande began working as a chambermaid. At the time, Clem spoke a little English, Rolande none.

In 1969, the Begins sold their farm and built a house near the Chateau on a lot that Tague had given them. There they raised two daughters: Lucy, who is now a pharmacist, and Chantal, a psychologist.

Clem went to work for Tague's construction company in 1970 and bought it two years later, renaming it Sugarloaf Construction. He developed his first subdivision, in Kingfield, in 1973. He went on to build housing developments in Farmington, Madison, Skowhegan, Stratton, and Wilton. In Carrabassett Valley, he built Village South, Gondola Village, Snowbrook Condominiums, Bigelow Townhouses, some units near the Glades, and—in just five days—the Touring Center (since renamed Outdoor Center). Rolande managed the books and administrative work. She also had her own drapery business with four employees.

The Begins have long been engaged in civic affairs. Clem was a Carrabassett Planning Board member for twelve years. He has served on the CVA and Bell Chapel boards of directors, the Franklin Memorial Hospital advisory board, and the Franklin County Soil and Water conservation board. He built the Anti-Gravity Complex and, because the budget was tight, worked for several months without compensation.

When the Begins announced their $1.75 million in donations at a charity banquet in 2010, attendees were stunned. Each donation was given as a matching gift, Clem said, "to inspire others to make gifts and support the community." The gifts included $1 million to the then-fledgling Maine Huts & Trails; $520,000 to Carrabassett Valley Academy's campus project; $170,000 to the Carrabassett Valley Public Library and Community Center; and $60,000 to the Sugarloaf Mountain Ski Club to help build the Bill & Joan Alfond Competition Center.

"My family's philanthropic priorities are health care, education, and tourism," Begin later told the *Irregular*. "Each one of the organizations we support plays a vital role in our community, Franklin County, and in Maine. We are choosing to give now because we want to see our gifts at work."

13

Institutions, Outdoor Recreation, and Partnerships

WITH NO AILING TRADITIONAL ECONOMY TO REINVENT, NO LAID-OFF workforce to reemploy, and no "but-we've-always-done-it-this-ways" to stymie ideas, Carrabassett Valley residents have embraced innovative projects, both public and private, since the beginning of the ski era. After municipal incorporation in 1972, they honed a clear sense of direction and a distinctive identity as a community built on outdoor recreation. They've been willing to think outside the box to fulfill that vision and to create the institutions, facilities, and services that make for a well-rounded community.

INSTITUTIONS

Carrabassett Valley Academy

Carrabassett Valley Academy is Maine's first ski and snowboard academy and one of around ten full-year ski-racing academies in the United States. It's an athletic-training school for serious snow competitors that, as of 2023, counts twelve Olympians and thirty-nine U.S. Ski Team members among its alumni. It's also a rigorous prep school, with a class schedule synced to students' training programs and teachers who adapt lessons for athletes on the road. Many graduates go on to colleges that are highly ranked for both academics and ski racing, such as Middlebury and Dartmouth.

"Competitive skiing and snowboarding take a lot of time and require a lot of travel," said head of school Kate Webber Punderson, a CVA alum whose parents, Peter and Martha Webber, are among the school's founders. "Our students have to miss a lot of class, but they have to keep up with their academics. A lot of them come here because traditional schools aren't set up to support elite athletes—they don't allow them to miss school for competitions. CVA is designed for that. Our students aren't sacrificing their education or their sport."

The school enrolls 115 students in grades 7–12, around 60 percent of them from Maine, the rest from other parts of the country and overseas. Applicants are required to submit academic records, essays, and recommendations from coaches and teachers. They typically spend a day at the school demonstrating their ski or snowboarding skills and otherwise getting acquainted. "CVA is a competitive school," Punderson said. "It's not a place to come and just have fun skiing." CVA also has a weekend program enrolling nearly 160 skiers. The school is Carrabassett Valley's second-largest employer, with sixty-five full-time employees.

The twenty-two-acre campus at the foot of Sugarloaf Mountain is named for King Cummings, a founding trustee and funder. It includes the seventeen-thousand-square-foot Peter and Martha Webber Academic Center and, connected to it by a common area, the dorm. There's a soccer field and running track. Students train on Sugarloaf's slopes and in the Anti-Gravity Complex.

The academy's roots are in the Sugarloaf Ski Club. In the 1960s, the club's junior racing program had grown to include freestyle, and more than 150 youngsters were training with their coaches every weekend, competing across New England and qualifying for national events. In 1969, some of the club's directors and race committee members formed the nonprofit Sugarloaf Regional Ski Educational Foundation to financially assist competitors with their travel demands. Three years later, the foundation added an academic tutorial program—the first ever approved by the State Department of Education. Jean Luce and Ginny Bousum worked with the state to develop a prospectus and, in Luce's words, "then conspired to get enough financial backers to convince King Cummings

A CVA student in freestyle competition. COURTESY OF CARRABASSETT VALLEY ACADEMY

to lead a board of directors. Ginny was the lobbyist and buffer to all those who tried to convince us the concept wouldn't work."

In fact, the concept proved itself quickly. High school students spent one week each month during the winter at Sugarloaf, training and being tutored in their school assignments. They also were tutored while away at competitions. Over the next decade, enrollment grew from nine to more than thirty-five students.

Meanwhile, in Vermont, the country's first three ski academies were taking root. Burke Mountain Academy (1970), Stratton Mountain School (1972), and Green Mountain Valley School (1973) served as models for what worked—and what didn't—when the Sugarloaf Regional Ski Educational Foundation decided to take its program to the next level. In 1982, Carrabassett Valley Academy opened as a five-month winter-term program. Classes were held in the basement of the Richard H. Bell Interfaith Chapel (then the Sugarloaf Interfaith Chapel), and the twenty-five students lived with their parents or teachers in condominiums on the mountain. Bruce Colon, who had directed alpine skiing at Northwood School

A CVA teacher helps a student with an assignment.
COURTESY OF CARRABASSETT VALLEY ACADEMY

in Lake Placid, was headmaster. The following year, with nearly double the enrollment, CVA purchased its own home: the Capricorn Lodge, which was renovated to house six classrooms, dormitories, a cafeteria/meeting hall, an office, a weight room, and a ski-preparation room.

After he arrived as headmaster in 1986–1987, John Ritzo worked with trustees and staff to revise the CVA's long-range plan, which led to the school's accreditation by the New England Association of Schools and Colleges in 1991. Under Ritzo's leadership, the school became the first ski academy in the nation to add snowboarding to its athletics program. "Within the first decade of CVA's existence, it had become an institution well recognized in both the college world of admissions officers and in international ski competition," Jean Luce wrote in a 2001 history submitted as part of CVA's recertification application to the New England Association of Schools and Colleges. "It was an institution producing highly motivated student athletes who were well-grounded achievers. CVA students were readily accepted by the top colleges in the U.S. and winning National Championship, World Championship, and even Olympic medals. The mission statement of providing a balance of academics and athletics was proving itself well."

Warren Cook, chairman of CVA's board of trustees at that time, focused on financial growth and stability, including the establishment of an endowment. Mark Fawcett, the first snowboard competitor to attend the school, challenged his fellow alumni by donating his prize money to the school.

Three years after partnering with the town to build the Anti-Gravity Complex, CVA purchased land from Sugarloaf and went on to build the campus. Capricorn Lodge is now used for faculty housing, offices, and meals, though plans call for a dining hall to be built adjacent to the dorms.

The $2.1 million Bill and Joan Alfond Competition Center (the school's collaboration with Sugarloaf and the Sugarloaf Ski Club) opened in 2016. In 2022, CVA, Sugarloaf, and Sugarloaf's owner, Boyne Resorts, again joined forces on the Podium Project, aimed at improving athletes' slalom and freestyle aerial performances. The project encompassed the addition of a high-speed T-bar and state-of-the-art snowmaking for the side-by-side training and racing trails Narrow Gauge and Competition Hill (as it did with the competition center, the town contributed $100,000 to this project). "The partnerships in this community are incredible," Punderson said. "We wouldn't exist without them."

Carrabassett Valley Public Library and Community Center

When town dignitaries plunged gold-plated shovels into the dirt off Carrabassett Drive on May 26, 2009, several people remarked that their wish was coming true. None had held that hope longer than Joyce Demshar. "It has been a dream of mine over the last 40 years for the town of Carrabassett Valley to have a library we can all be proud of," Demshar remarked that day. The groundbreaking was the culmination of "hard work, faith, hope, and contributions," she said. "I am proud to be a member of this far-seeing community."

Joyce Demshar started the book collection that became Carrabassett Valley Public Library in the early 1970s. Back then, her name was

The library's distinctive entry is a nod to Carrabassett Valley's lumbering heritage.
COURTESY OF CARRABASSETT VALLEY PUBLIC LIBRARY

Joyce Peters, and she juggled three jobs—insurance agency manager, town clerk, and newspaper typesetter—in an office at Valley Crossing Shopping Center. The nascent library was a bookcase stocked with donated paperbacks on the landing outside her door. It had no catalog and no budget. People simply borrowed books with a promise to return them. When they did, they often came with a few new titles for the collection.

After the shopping center was dismantled and moved to the mountain in 1977, the books were packed up and stowed, and Demshar arranged to work temporarily at the Chateau des Tagues bar. Meanwhile, town manager Preston Jordan and his wife, Gail, were finishing their new house on Carrabassett Valley Drive. There, in the Jordans' basement, the town government and library found their next accommodations. John and Caroline Rogers (parents of Ed, Frank, and Bob of Red Stallion fame) built some shelves in a small backroom and cataloged the paperbacks. The Carrabassett Valley Public Library was born, but it still had no budget.

That didn't come until March 1989, when town meeting voters supported expanding and finding a permanent home for the book collection and establishing a slate of library services. By late October, the library had settled into the former Mountain Tops T-shirt factory next to the Jordans' house. It shared the space—and some of its board members—with the now-defunct Western Maine Children's Museum.

At first, the library was open only on Mondays, with librarian Kathie Tibbetts at the check-out desk. The trustees, chaired by Nancy Marshall, created programs, like family film nights and children's story hours. They scoured the community for equipment donations, such as a film projector, VCR, photocopy machine, and computer. And they bought books, beginning with a set of hardcover classics purchased with town funds and a Library of America grant.

In 1991, Andrea "Andie" DeBiase—then Andie Johnson—became the first library director. A preschool teacher from Falmouth, DeBiase had applied for the position of children's museum coordinator. "After the interview, a board member said they were also looking for someone to be a part-time coordinator of the library, and would I be interested in doing that as well," DeBiase recalled in 2022, her thirty-first year as library director. "I told them I didn't know how long I'd be here. They asked me if I could commit to a year, and I said I could. Then a couple of board members, longtime Sugarloafers, elbowed each other and said, 'That's what I said 15 years ago.' Carrabassett Valley grows on you. When you first move here, you may feel as though you're in the middle of nowhere, and before you know it, it becomes home."

DeBiase not only accepted both jobs but also took over the preschool program run by museum founder Karen White in the same building. In 1998, when she was expecting her first child, she withdrew from the museum coordinator job and focused exclusively on her preschool, a Montessori-based program for three- to five-year-olds, and on the library, which, with two thousand books and a growing membership eager for more services, had outgrown its space. DeBiase and the library board began researching the feasibility of building a new library.

In 2006, with voters' approval, selectmen appointed a New Building Committee to gather residents' input and develop a proposal. They envisioned a lodge with a warm wood interior—or, as DeBiase put it, "a living room for the community, with a fireplace!" It would have a common room

Library story hour takes place around the play ship built by the late Dutch Demshar.
COURTESY OF CARRABASSETT VALLEY PUBLIC LIBRARY

for socializing, a community room for programs and events, and a rental space for a private childcare center. At its core, it would be a resource for information and internet access. The committee presented the plan to the town with a commitment to raise private funds to cover some of the projected $1.2 million cost.

Library board president Jean Keith and volunteer grant writer Kimberley Kearing led a capital campaign that ultimately raised $540,000 from private donations, grants, and events. The town contributed the rest, taking some of the money from the recreation endowment fund. The building site adjacent to the Anti-Gravity Complex was cobbled together with land donations from Sugarloaf (and its then-owner, CNL Lifestyle Properties), Mountainside Grocers, and Carrabassett Valley Academy.

The library opened in February 2010. Its design, by Portland architectural firm Reed & Company, reflects both Carrabassett Valley's lumbering heritage and its modernity. Built by Linwood Doble Custom Home

Builders, the two-story flat-roofed center structure is distinguished by a covered entry with a truss constructed of full-length pine logs. The roof pitches steeply downward over the north and south wings, the former clad in brick-red shingles, the other in similarly stained clapboards. The central entrance hall comprises two seating areas and wall space for art exhibits. The library in the west wing includes a reading area with large stone fireplace and a children's area with a play ship built by Dutch Demshar. The north wing contains the Western Maine Center for Children, a nonprofit childcare facility and successor to the children's museum. Off the entrance hall is a community room named for Rolande and Clem Begin, who donated $170,000 to the library construction. It opens onto a patio composed of "Forever Stones" purchased by donors and engraved with names and messages.

The community garden on the south-facing grassy area next to the library grows food for people in need. Volunteers built six raised beds in 2014 with materials donated by local businesses. Today around twenty

The community garden. COURTESY OF CARRABASSETT VALLEY PUBLIC LIBRARY

people are involved, whether planting, weeding, watering, and harvesting organic vegetables or driving the produce to food banks that serve local people in need. "It's so typical of this community," said library president Pink Slagle, who initially suggested the garden's altruistic mission. "Most things accomplished here are a conglomerate effort. No one is worried about getting credit. They just come together and get it done to benefit the community."

When the library broke ground on its new building, it had five hundred members. Within two years of the building's completion, that number had quadrupled. As of 2022, there were more than five thousand members. "Every single person who comes in says it's a beautiful building, and they're glad we're here," DeBiase said. "I think it adds to the quality of life in an immeasurable way."

Maine Ski and Snowboard Museum

The Maine Ski and Snowboard Museum delves into the state's skiing and snowboarding history at its home on the Sugarloaf Access Road, in traveling exhibits and installations, and on its website, which is rich with slideshows, oral histories, and documentaries. Presentations have included such topics as *Made in Maine*, focusing on manufacturers of skis, snowboards, boots, and other equipment; *Winter Carnivals in Maine*, a look at multi-day celebrations in various towns; *Five Centuries of Snowboarding*, about the development of the sport; *Stories about Women in Skiing*, chronicling the history of women who have advanced the sport; and *Why We Ski*, which explored exactly that.

Founded as the Ski Museum of Maine in 1995 by a group of friends from the Sugarloaf Ski Club, the organization was later incorporated as a nonprofit with a board of directors led by Jean Luce. It obtained a grant to contract with an archivist, accession artifacts and documents, and purchase archival storage boxes. Megan Roberts of Farmington was the first executive director.

The museum has had several homes. It started out in a small building on Route 27 owned by the town of Carrabassett Valley; then it moved to donated space in Farmington and again to donated space in Kingfield. It opened a satellite gallery at the Bethel Historical Society in 2018 and converted two exhibits (*Maine Olympians* and *Mountains of Maine*) into mobile exhibits.

In 2022, the museum moved to its current home on the Access Road, a process that led to the rediscovery of many photos, maps, and news clippings in need of accessioning and preservation. Its four-person staff includes executive director Kate Barnes, curator Karen Campbell, bookkeeper Leslie Norton, and researcher Bob Bailiee.

Richard H. Bell Interfaith Chapel and Sugarloaf Area Christian Ministry

If you believe, as many do, that a church is not a building, but rather the people who are gathered within, then the Richard H. Bell Interfaith Chapel came into being in the early 1960s. That's when Kingfield United Methodist Church pastor Charles Reid began preaching to skiers in the basement of the Sugarloaf base lodge (they wore their Sunday best—parkas and puffy pants). After seeing a chapel at a New Hampshire ski area in 1962, congregant and Sugarloaf founding director Dick Bell proposed creating a dedicated space where people could pray and reflect without the *clomp-clomp-clomp* of ski boots overhead. He made his pitch to the

The Revs. Earle and Pam Morse of Sugarloaf Area Christian Ministry lead services at "the AMP," an amphitheater on Sugarloaf outfitted with a stage and benches. Parishioners arrive by SuperQuad. AUTHOR

Sugarloaf Ski Club that fall, and the drive was on to build what was then called Sugarloaf Interfaith Chapel.

The first fundraising phase paid for construction of a heated enclosed foundation adjacent to the resort's parking lot on the mountain's lower northeast slope. Worshipers gathered there from 1965 until 1968, when the chapel was completed and the nonprofit organization Sugarloaf Interfaith Chapel, Inc. was formed. With its expansive, steeply pitched roof and rustic, unfinished wood interior, the chapel references the hundreds of A-frames that sprang up in the valley in the 1960s. Its cost—around $70,000—had been paid almost entirely by skiers and other members of the Sugarloaf community.

In January 1974, the chapel's directors renamed the building for their ailing treasurer, Bell, who not only had been the prime mover behind the project but also was a beloved figure on the mountain and in northern Franklin County. Besides his involvement in Sugarloaf's founding, Bell had served as director of the Farmington Ski Club and the Maine Ski Council. As vice president of the U.S. Eastern Amateur Ski Association, he led the campaign to require junior competitors to wear protective headgear in USEASA-sanctioned races. At the time of the chapel dedication, he'd recently retired from his Farmington insurance agency due to illness. He died the next month. His daughter, Elizabeth "Buffy" Bell-Folsom, succeeded him as treasurer, a position she still holds.

Bell and his co-founders felt strongly that the chapel should be interfaith and open to all. At first, three types of services were held every week during the winter ski season—Catholic, Episcopalian, and nondenominational Protestant—but, by the late 1970s, services were being offered only around Christmas and Easter. In 1982, the Reverend Skip Schwartz, Charles Reid's successor, helped form Sugarloaf Area Christian Ministry and restarted the season-long schedule at the chapel.

Earle and Pam Morse, who took over the ministry in 1990, introduced year-round interdenominational services and have responded creatively to the interests of their parishioners, many of whom are weekenders who want to get the most out of their lift tickets. From Christmas through Easter, the Morses offer Downhill Worship: attendees meet at the base of the Double Runner chair and take a run down the mountain,

The Richard H. Bell Interfaith Chapel was built 1965–1968, but the congregation is older, having initially gathered in the Sugarloaf base lodge. AUTHOR

stopping four times for prayer and reflection. In summer, the Morses lead services in "the AMP," an outdoor amphitheater outfitted with a stage and benches at the top of the SuperQuad lift.

In addition to Sugarloaf Area Ministry, Our Lady of the Lakes provides Catholic Mass at the chapel from December 1 through Palm Sunday. The chapel hosts weddings, funerals, celebrations of life, counseling meetings, Carrabassett Valley Academy graduation exercises, and other events. The Sugarloaf Ski Patrol headquarters is in the basement. The family room—a later addition—is named for Clem Begin, a generous donor and former board president.

RECREATION FACILITIES AND ORGANIZATIONS

Adaptive Outdoor Education Center

The Adaptive Outdoor Education Center is an outgrowth of founders Bruce and Annemarie Albiston's work with the Aphasia Center of Maine, which provides recreational, educational, and emotional support to people with aphasia and their families. Built in 2015 on a two-acre site leased from the town, AOEC offers low-cost lodging for people with disabilities and their families, a "challenge playground," and an accessible nature trail. The Albistons set out to make a difference in the lives of people with disabilities after Annemarie's father, Andre, had a stroke and acquired aphasia, affecting his speech and language. The Carrabassett lodge is now one of three AOEC campuses in Maine.

Anti-Gravity Complex

Gravity is no less a force inside the Anti-Gravity Complex, but the facility does provide the equipment for athletes to defy it for a few seconds at least. Shared by the town of Carrabassett Valley and CVA, the twenty-thousand-square-foot gym is home to two Olympic-size trampolines, Maine's largest indoor skate park, a climbing wall (named for—you guessed it—Clem Begin), a multi-purpose court, a track, and a weight room. Former CVA headmaster John Ritzo summed it up at the building's dedication in 2001: "From a world-class athlete to a private citizen who just wants to do a simple workout, this recreation center has it all." The complex is open to the public whenever CVA athletes are not training.

Bill & Joan Alfond Competition Center

Sugarloaf Mountain has tested the skills of elite skiers and snowboarders in hundreds of competitions since the first Giant Sugar Slalom in 1952. In 2016, Sugarloaf, the Sugarloaf Ski Club, and Carrabassett Valley Academy raised the level of their programs with the opening of the Bill & Joan Alfond Competition Center, located just downhill from the Narrow Gauge race course. The building is the competition and events headquarters for all three organizations and serves as a welcome center for competing athletes and their coaches.

Bill and Joan Alfond, whose families have skied at Sugarloaf for generations, gave a $1 million grant for the center's construction through their foundation. The town of Carrabassett Valley, CVA supporters, Sugarloaf, and members of the ski club contributed the remaining $1.1 million. Longtime Sugarloafers Rick Goduti and Maggie Stanley, of Portland-based Goduti-Thomas Architects, designed the contemporary-rustic structure, borrowing structural elements from the gondola station that once stood on the same site. The building contains a great room with gas fireplace, warming kitchen, and cafe tables; offices for the ski club and for Sugarloaf and CVA competition staff; dedicated team rooms for the Colby College and University of Maine at Farmington ski teams; a tuning/waxing facility; a trainers' room; and a workshop for equipment repair.

Carrabassett Region Chapter of the New England Mountain Biking Association (CR-NEMBA)

NEMBA is a nonprofit recreational trails advocacy organization with thirty-three chapters throughout New England and over seven thousand members. In addition to contributing thousands of volunteer hours toward building and maintaining the Carrabassett Valley Trails network, the Carrabassett chapter leads group rides and holds skills clinics and trail-building schools. It was founded in 2010 to fulfill one of the recommendations contained in the International Mountain Bike Association's report to the town of Carrabassett Valley.

Carrabassett Valley ATV Club

In 2010, Carrabassett Valley Outdoor Association members Neal Trask and John McCatherin recruited a handful of fellow ATV riders to help build a multi-use recreational bridge across the Carrabassett River. Soon after, the group organized as a club and developed nearly twenty-five miles of trails that first year.

Carrabassett Valley Outdoor Association/ Neal Trask Range

Created in 2000 to encourage "in every possible way the proper use and conservation of the region," CVOA now boasts more than eleven hundred members. Every year, the club organizes dozens of outings around bicycling, camping, canoeing, fishing, hiking, kayaking, and snowshoeing, as well as a few trips to ski resorts out west and in Canada and Europe. The late Neal Trask, a CVOA founder, developed the thirty-acre shooting range that bears his name. Members participate in the annual town-sponsored Route 27 cleanup and a club-sponsored cleanup of hiking trails, including sections of the AT.

Carrabassett Valley Trails

This mountain bike/Nordic skiing trail network, located primarily within the town of Carrabassett Valley, comprises roughly eighty miles and continues to be developed by Carrabassett Valley Trails Committee, whose members include representatives from the town, Carrabassett Region NEMBA, Maine Huts & Trails, and Sugarloaf. The Outdoor Center is the primary trailhead, with parking, trail maps, a bike-wash station, and Allspeed Cyclery and Snow, a shop offering bike rentals and service. Trails wind through the Outdoor Center property, up Sugarloaf Mountain, and north to Maine Huts & Trails' Stratton Brook Hut. The signature trail is arguably the smooth and easy Narrow Gauge Pathway, which provides access to several single-tracks, including Caboose, Camel Humps, and Crockertown, as well as to Poplar Falls Hut.

J. V. Wing Snowmobile Club

Formed in 1987, the J. V. Wing Snowmobile Club maintains and grooms fifty-five miles of trails that are part of the 134-mile Black Fly Loop. The club makes many contributions to the community that are unrelated to snowmobiling, such as grooming the Narrow Gauge Pathway for cross-country skiing and the Special Olympics softball tournament field.

Maine Huts & Trails

MH&T maintains four wilderness lodges strung out along an eighty-mile trail network: Stratton Brook Hut and Poplar Hut in Carrabassett Valley, Flagstaff Hut on the east shore of Flagstaff Lake in Carrying Place Township, and Grand Falls Hut in West Forks. They're the partially realized dream of Larry Warren and the Western Mountains Foundation, who first introduced the concept of a trail hut system in 1977.

Opened between 2008 and 2012, the off-the-grid lodges have bunk-rooms, renewable energy–powered heating systems, and bathrooms with running water and hot showers. Initially, caretakers prepared meals for guests during the Nordic ski season, and the commercial kitchens were open on a self-serve basis during the off-season. MH&T received abundant good press, but revenues consistently fell short. In 2019, the non-profit announced that rising costs and staff shortages were threatening its ability to open the huts and groom trails. That winter, the huts operated on a self-service basis. They were closed in 2020 due to the COVID-19 pandemic. In 2021 and 2022, MH&T employed a new business model at the Stratton Brook, Poplar, and Flagstaff huts, offering different services depending on the season and day of the week.

Western Mountains Foundation spent years negotiating with land-owners over trail and hut locations, including a route through Bigelow Preserve, which was staunchly opposed by Friends of Bigelow. Warren initially envisioned twelve huts on a 180-mile trail system stretching from Bethel to Greenville.

The Outdoor Center

The town-owned and Sugarloaf-managed Outdoor Center is the hub of an eighty-mile trail network for cross-country skiing, fat biking, and mountain biking. It also has an NHL-size skating rink and a lodge with bike- and ski-rental shops and a cafe.

The center is the town of Carrabassett Valley's first creatively financed recreation project, paid for in part with money from the recreation facilities endowment fund. Initially called the Touring Center, it opened in 1976 with forty miles of Nordic trails. Today, it's Maine's largest Nordic center.

Special Olympics Maine Winter Games

Five hundred athletes from across the state compete in the annual Special Olympics Maine Winter Games at Sugarloaf. The three-day event, supported by three hundred volunteers, includes competitions in Nordic, alpine, and seated skiing; snowshoeing; and figure and speed skating. The games open with what may be the state's biggest potluck supper, held in the base lodge. Sugarloafers and residents from Carrabassett Valley and surrounding towns prepare hundreds of casseroles and desserts for the athletes, coaches, and their families—upward of eight hundred people. Volunteers also make and bag thousands of sandwiches to be distributed to teams each day of competition. Maine became the first state to hold a winter Special Olympics when Kiwanis Ski Slope in Gorham hosted events in 1970. Sugarloaf has hosted the games since 1982.

Sugarloaf Golf Club

Anyone who golfs in Maine knows about Sugarloaf Golf Club. Owned by the town and operated by Sugarloaf resort, the 107-acre course is a fixture on national magazine best-course lists, and it has a reputation for being difficult. "Its fairways are invariably enfolded in dense, untamed forest, and the first six holes on the back nine weave precariously back and forth across the South Branch of the Carrabassett River," writes Stephen E. Abbott in *Maine* magazine. "For the average golfer who happens to be playing poorly,

COURTESY OF SUGARLOAF

an 18-hole round can quickly build, crescendo-like, into a veritable kettle-drum-pounding, cymbal-crashing symphony of lost balls.... Yes, Sugarloaf is a tough course, but it's also fair and—in the parlance of golfers—exceedingly playable. More to the point, it's just plain fun."

What truly sets Sugarloaf Golf Club apart, however, is its wilderness setting, says John DeBiase, who has worked at the club since it opened in 1985. The course was carved out of Sugarloaf Mountain's forested west slope, and its architect, Robert Trent Jones Jr., designed each hole to be visually isolated from the others. "Most other golf courses are laid out and open—you can see people in the other fairway, or you might be close to someone on a tee," DeBiase says. "That doesn't happen here. It's very quiet. You're on your own on the fairway." Every hole has a mountain view, be it Sugarloaf, Burnt, the Bigelow Range, or Crocker Cirque. Sightings of moose, white-tailed deer, and even bears are common. Holes 10–15 are called "the string of pearls" for their exceptional setting along the Carrabassett River. The course's signature hole is number 11, the Precipice, distinguished for its dramatic 124-foot drop-off from tee to green.

Sugarloaf Ski Club

It's not a stretch to say that the town of Carrabassett Valley owes its existence to the Sugarloaf Ski Club. In 1950, the club's founders cut Sugarloaf's first ski trails and built the first stretch of the Access Road. A few years later, a group of club members formed the Sugarloaf Mountain Corporation, which transformed the rugged upstart of a ski mountain into one of New England's top ski resorts. Other ski club offspring include Carrabassett Valley Academy and the Maine Ski and Snowboard Museum.

Throughout its history, the club has organized competitive ski meets, beginning with the 1952 Giant Sugar Slalom, in which skiers hiked or skinned to the Snowfields and raced down Winter's Way. Today, with fourteen hundred members, it continues to work with Sugarloaf in running competitions like the Freestyle and Alpine National Championships, NCAA Championships, Snowboard Grand Prix, and World Junior Championships. The club raised $120,000 to build the Jean Luce Competition Timing Building and contributed $200,000 (raised through cookouts, raffles, and other events) to the construction of the Bill & Joan

Alfond Competition Center. Each year, the club awards several thousand dollars in scholarships to young ski and snowboard competitors.

SUGARLOAF AMBULANCE & RESCUE AND NORTHSTAR EMS

Ron Morin earned the nickname "grandfather of Maine EMS" for the pioneering work he performed at Sugarloaf Ambulance & Rescue, the service he founded at the foot of Sugarloaf Mountain in the 1970s. Under Morin's direction for twenty-eight years, Sugarloaf Ambulance & Rescue not only responded to medical emergencies but also designed and built ambulances for emergency medical services around the state.

After a mid-1960s stint in the navy, where his duties included driving the ambulance, Morin returned to his native Livermore Falls. In 1969, he suffered serious burns in an apartment fire and endured a long wait for the local ambulance. After the service's owner apologetically explained that he'd been short-staffed, Morin applied for the job and became a state-licensed ambulance attendant.

In 1971, he took an EMT course at Harvard Medical School. "I was so excited, I asked, how do I bring this to state of Maine?" Morin recalled in an interview with Blaine Bacon on Bacon's YouTube program, *Mr. Bacon's Neighborhood*. Harvard allowed Morin to teach EMT at the University of Maine at Farmington in coordination with Dr. Paul Brinkman. Morin also launched Sugarloaf Ambulance & Rescue and offered first-responder courses there.

In 1982, Morin and seventeen other students enrolled in Maine's new EMS training program and graduated as the state's first licensed paramedics. He served as Carrabassett Valley's fire chief for seventeen years, was a member of the Maine EMS Board, and founded the Maine EMS Honor Guard.

The best part of being a paramedic, Morin told the *Sun Journal* in 2015, is "caring, giving comfort, preventing the sudden onset of death, holding mémère's hand at one time and getting into the craziest positions extricating someone from a crushed vehicle the next, watching someone go from near death and paralysis to walking into your office and saying, 'Thank you.'"

In 1996, Morin sold the EMS portion of the business to Peter Boucher, who in turn sold it a few years later to Franklin Memorial Hospital, which merged it into NorthStar EMS, a regional service with bases in Carrabassett Valley, Farmington, Livermore Falls, Phillips, and Rangeley.

Every year, NorthStar responds to over 5,500 emergency and medical calls in a 2,800-square-mile area. In Carrabassett Valley, it boosts its regular twenty-four-hours-a-day service with an additional ambulance on weekends and vacations during the ski season.

SUGARLOAF REGIONAL AIRPORT

Developed by Franklin County on the grassy air strip that belonged to Leo Tague, Sugarloaf Regional Airport opened in late 1968 with a 2,800-foot paved runway designed to handle light twin-engine aircraft. In 1985, when county commissioners wanted to build an airport capable of handling larger planes, they sold Sugarloaf Regional to Carrabassett Valley for $100. The town immediately extended the runway and has since gone on to make numerous improvements, including enlarged taxiways, navigational updates, and, in 2022, the construction of ten tee-hangars for storage of private aircraft. The airport is home to two flight schools, and it hosts an annual fly-in that attracts about thirty airplanes.

Planes on the Sugarloaf Regional Airport tarmac, with the Bigelow range looming behind. COURTESY OF TOM WALLACE

CARRABASSETT VALLEY SANITARY DISTRICT (LET IT SNOW . . . FLUENT!)

The Carrabassett Valley Sanitary District was the first municipal waste-water authority in the world to dispose of wastewater by turning it into snow. The process, called *freeze nucleation* and branded as Snowfluent, works on the same principle as snowmaking machines: atomizing nozzles spray wastewater under high pressure into cold air, where it immediately freezes. The resultant "snow" is then pumped over a forested area, where it melts and seeps into the ground in spring and early summer.

The district started making Snowfluent soon after it took over Sugartech, Sugarloaf's wastewater treatment operation, a key component of the town of Carrabassett Valley's 1993 debt-reduction plan for the resort. Sugartech disposed of the treated effluent by conventional spray irrigation, which involves showering it over a designated area. Wastewater produced in winter had to be held in seven clay-lined lagoons until spring, and by then their combined thirty-eight-million-gallon capacity would be maxed out. Based on the resort's development ambitions and state Department of Environmental Protection requirements, Sugarloaf's engineers had forecast the need for as many as fifty-one lagoons, at a cost of $250,000 each, and twenty-six spray irrigation areas, at a cost of $200,000 each, according to Larry Warren, one of the original three sanitary district trustees.

Warren proposed that the district adopt a system that could disperse wastewater in winter, thus reducing the number of lagoons required to hold it. He knew the firm that could build it: Delta Engineering, the Canadian manufacturer of Sugarloaf's snowmaking equipment. Delta had already developed a method for turning effluent into snow for an Arctic research station, and it was testing a similar system for an Ontario ski resort.

DEP regulators were open to granting a permit for Snowfluent in Carrabassett Valley, but they had some concerns. Although the district had supplied the DEP with Canada Ministry of Environment data showing that volatile gases, bacteria, and other disease-causing organisms weren't present at the Ontario test site, no one could explain what had happened to them. DEP wanted the answer.

The district selected the Portland engineering firm Woodard & Curran to analyze the technology. The engineers found that the high-pressure freezing process caused cell-wall rupture of bacteria, rendering them harmless. Nitrogen, carbon gases, and hydrogen sulfide were released into the atmosphere. While the snow ages, the ammonia evaporates and the dissolved ammonium salts—mostly phosphate—precipitate. Snow-fluent, in other words, is as pure as the driven snow, maybe even purer. Of course, it isn't really snow. Like all machine-made snow, it consists of dense tiny beads of ice, not the airy complex crystalline structures of natural snow. DEP allowed the project to move forward.

Today the Carrabassett Valley Sanitary District serves thirteen hundred living units on the mountain, as well as Sugarloaf's commercial facilities. Wastewater flows by gravity through an eight-mile series of sewer mains to a pump station at the base of the ski area. It's then pumped 1.2 miles to the treatment facility on Bigelow Hill. Snowfluent is strictly a cold-weather technology, and the district begins using it as soon as the weather allows. The early snowpack keeps the ground from freezing, so when spring arrives, the melting effluent seeps into the ground with minimal runoff. The rest of the year, the district treats and disposes of wastewater through spray irrigation.

The Carrabassett Sanitary District spent about $750,000 to implement Snowfluent technology in 1994 and has made investments in equipment since, but it hasn't had to build any more lagoons. It paid off its debt from the Sugartech purchase within fifteen years and reduced the tie-in fee for new homes from $5,000 to $3,000, one of the lowest rates in the state.

SUGARLOAF EXPLORER

The nonprofit Western Maine Transportation Services operates the Sugarloaf Explorer shuttle system in collaboration with the town of Carrabassett Valley, Sugarloaf, the state of Maine, and owners of mountain properties. Ridership averages 145,000 passengers each ski season, mostly on the mountain, as well as limited service to other parts of town.

Created in 2007, Sugarloaf Explorer is the successor to a town/Sugarloaf shuttle system that was becoming increasingly expensive to operate. Modeled after shuttle services at other major ski areas, the Explorer's nonprofit status allows access to federal and state transportation funding to help pay for the service and equipment. Other contributions come from the town, Sugarloaf, and condo and homeowner association fees.

WSKI-TV 17

Sugarloaf's marketing department launched WSKI in 1979 as a closed-circuit station available only on the mountain. The resort shut down the station in 1986 when it filed for bankruptcy, but some of the crew continued as the independent Snowfields Productions, using equipment leased from Sugarloaf. Snowfields has since upgraded equipment and evolved into an essential service, offering live shows about regional events, interviews with local people, up-to-the-minute forecasts and trail reports, and programming from outside television. Carrabassett Valley contributes a portion of the station's franchise fees.

14

Epilogue—Looking Ahead

As Carrabassett Valley's sixth decade unfolds, development of new recreation facilities and homes is as brisk as ever.

Sugarloaf has embarked on what's been called its most transformative project in forty years: a 450-acre expansion on West Mountain, with alpine trails, a downhill mountain-bike park, and 196 dwellings, including single-family houses, duplexes, and condos.

The Carrabassett Valley Trails partners are expanding the mountain bike/Nordic ski trail network at a rate of two to three miles a year.

Sunrise in the valley. COURTESY OF JAMIE WALTER

Meanwhile, selectmen continue to seek negotiations with the Penobscot Nation to reopen access to trails on its land. The ideal agreement, according to selectman Lloyd Cuttler, would both support the tribe's quest for sovereignty and protect owners of homes abutting Penobscot land from incompatible development. A parallel effort is underway at the state level.

Carrabassett Valley's year-round population continues to grow. A number of seasonal-home owners retreated to Carrabassett Valley in 2020 and 2021 to wait out the COVID-19 pandemic. Precisely how many people came is unknown, but their presence was significant enough to be noticed by store and restaurant owners and by the school board, which reported a spike in enrollment. Also unknown is whether these transplants are here to stay, but the remote-work arrangements that make it possible for many of them provide a hint of how Carrabassett Valley's demographics might change over the next several years. Historically, the vast majority of year-round residents have worked in recreation-related jobs. With telecommuting, a wider variety of careers might be represented.

Like many towns in Maine, Carrabassett Valley saw its shortage of affordable housing exacerbated by the pandemic real-estate boom.

The Longfellow Range in fall. SAMUEL TRAFTON/MAINE DRONE IMAGING

Selectman John Beaupre leads a regional committee that is looking for workforce housing sites and exploring the creation of a nonprofit housing trust, which would have access to a broad range of public and private funds to develop affordable homes.

Carrabassett Valley, then, continues to evolve, but one thing remains unchanged: Its founders' vision of a community planned by its citizens around outdoor recreation is part of the town's DNA, a baked-in blueprint for growth and prosperity. Like town leaders everywhere, Carrabassett's selectmen, planners, and economic development officials seek ways to diversify and broaden the economic base, but they do it almost exclusively underneath the recreation umbrella. The strategy has solidified the town's identity as a destination for fun in a beautiful mountain wilderness.

CARRABASSETT VALLEY TIMELINE

13,000–10,000 BCE

—Paleo-Indians hunt and camp in the Carrabassett River Valley, leaving behind artifacts to be discovered by twenty-first-century archaeologists.

1724

—A Massachusetts Colony militia attacks the Abenakis' Norridgewock settlement at what is now Old Point in Madison. Captain Johnson Harmon identifies one of the twenty-six murdered Abenakis as "Captain Carabasset."

1793

—Philadelphia land speculator William Bingham purchases one million acres in the Upper Kennebec Valley.

1828

—Bingham's heirs sell 1,457 acres along both sides of the Carrabassett River, which are divided into fifteen settlers' lots located between the present-day site of Huse Mill Road and the Kingfield line. The first settlers arrive and begin logging.

—Stagecoach service begins between Kingfield and Eustis.

1830

—Skowhegan lawyer and dramatist Nathaniel Deering publishes *Carabasset or the Last of the Norridgewocks*, igniting interest in the

Norridgewock story. Over the next few decades, the name Carrabassett is given to everything from racehorses to boats.

1840

—Jerusalem's population is forty-seven; Crockertown's is six.

1855

—Township 3 Range 2 (Jerusalem) is officially organized and named Treadwell Plantation, but the incorporated status is brief.

1860–1862

—A section of the former Seven Mile River is labeled "Carrabassett River" for the first time on J. Chace Jr. & Co.'s groundbreaking state and county maps.

1880

—Jerusalem's population is twenty-one; Crockertown's is two.

1884

—The Strong-to-Kingfield line of the Franklin & Megantic (F&M) narrow-gauge railroad opens, leading to intensive logging and mill building in the Carrabassett River Valley.

1894

—The F&M extends its line from Kingfield to Carrabassett Station in Jerusalem.

1898

—The F&M extends its line to Bigelow, a lumbering village in Crockertown.

1900

—Jerusalem's population is thirty-five; Crockertown's also is thirty-five.

1902

—The newly formed Carrabassett Spring Mineral Company ships bottled water from the Carrabassett Spring Farm health retreat to Boston, where it's sold as a cure-all.

1908

—A fire, possibly started by sparks thrown from a train, burns 5,500 acres in Jerusalem and Crockertown. Hammond Pond Mountain is henceforth known as Burnt Mountain.

1910

—Jerusalem's population is twenty-seven; Crockertown's is forty-six.

1912

—William Record begins operating Record's Sporting Camps on seventy-five acres in Jerusalem, opposite the site of today's Sugar-Bowl bowling alley.

1925

—Rail service to Bigelow ceases.

1927

—State Highway 27 is built, linking Kingfield and Eustis.

1930

—Jerusalem's population is 185; Crockertown's is ten.

1935

—The F&M shuts down for good.

1940

—Jerusalem's population is forty-one; Crockertown's is thirty-seven.

1948

—Amos Winter and the Bigelow Boys ski Sugarloaf Mountain for the first time.

1949

—The newly formed Maine Ski Council identifies Sugarloaf as having the best potential for a ski resort.

1950

—The Sugarloaf Mountain Ski Club forms to build an access road to Sugarloaf and cut a trail that it names Winter's Way.

—Jerusalem's population is ten; Crockertown's is four.

1955

—A group of ski club members form the publicly held Sugarloaf Mountain Corporation to develop a large modern ski area at Sugarloaf.

1958

—The first ski-era lodging, Judson's Sugarloaf Motel, opens in Jerusalem.

1959

—Dave Rollins and Wes Sanborn build the first of the Carriage and Huston Brook roads A-frames.

1960

—Don and Maryann Pfeifle open the first on-mountain lodging: Sugarloaf Inn.

—Jerusalem's population is eleven; Crockertown's is not recorded.

1961

—Bigelow Corporation breaks ground on the first on-mountain housing development: Sugarloaf Village.

—A fire destroys part of Tagues' Motel. In just a few months, Leo Tague opens a new and fancier one, Chateau des Tagues.

1962

—Après-ski legend Red Stallion Inn opens just after midnight on January 1 in Dead River Company's former horse barn. Singer/humorist Jud Strunk is on stage.

1963

—The state legislature changes the name of Crockertown to Sugarloaf Township.

1967

—Franklin County purchases Leo Tague's airstrip and adjoining plots and develops Sugarloaf Regional Airport.

1969

—Construction of the Richard H. Bell Interfaith Chapel is completed.

1969

—Red Stallion regulars organize a party at the dump for a visiting *Playboy* reporter and photographer. It's featured in the magazine's November 1969 issue.

1970

—Mountainside Real Estate breaks ground on Maine's first condominium development.

1971

—Dead River Company executive Chris Hutchins urges residents of Jerusalem, Sugarloaf, and Wyman townships to form a new town.
—Sugarloaf hosts the Alpine Skiing World Cup, bringing international attention to the fledgling resort.

1972

—The former Jerusalem Township incorporates as the town of Carrabassett Valley.
—Sugarloaf builds Village Center, the first base village at a ski area in the East.
—The Maine Department of Transportation designates Route 27 a scenic highway.

1974

—Carrabassett Valley's property tax rate of $8.30 per thousand valuation is the lowest in Maine.

1975

—Carrabassett Valley annexes Sugarloaf Township. The combined town establishes the recreation facilities endowment fund, which will be used to finance numerous recreation projects in the future.

1976

—The nonprofit Western Mountains Corporation develops the town-owned Touring Center (now Outdoor Center). It's Carrabassett Valley's first public/private recreation project.

1977

—Larry Warren, Tom Hildreth, and Lloyd Cuttler acquire Valley Crossing Shopping Center from Dead River Company and move it to the mountain, where it's renamed Village West.

1980

—Carrabassett Valley's population is 107.

1981

—Dead River Company sells all of its Carrabassett Valley land to the Penobscot Nation. The land totals about twenty-four thousand acres, which is roughly half the town.

—Jud Strunk and store owner Dick Ayotte are killed in a plane crash shortly after takeoff from Sugarloaf Regional Airport.

1982

—Carrabassett Valley Academy is established. It opens in the basement of the Richard H. Bell Interfaith Chapel and moves into the former Capricorn Lodge the next year.

—Sugarloaf hosts the Maine Special Olympics Winter Games for the first time.

1983

—The new town office is completed at a cost of $35,000. The adjacent town park costs $38,000.

1985

—Sugarloaf Golf Club opens. It's the product of a partnership between Carrabassett Valley, Sugarloaf, and developer Peter Webber.

1986

—Sugarloaf files for Chapter 11 bankruptcy protection.

1987

—A reorganized Sugarloaf emerges from bankruptcy protection.

—The *Virgin Atlantic Flyer* sets a world distance record for hot-air balloons with its 2,900-mile flight from Carrabassett Valley to Ireland.

1990

—Carrabassett Valley's population is 325.

1993

—The Carrabassett Valley annual town meeting votes 74–4 in favor of a plan to help Sugarloaf reduce its debt.

1999

—Longtime Sugarloafers pack the shuttered Red Stallion for Sugarloaf Founder's Night. (See archival footage online at wskitv.com.)

2000

—Carrabassett Valley's population is 399.

2001

—Carrabassett Valley partners with Carrabassett Valley Academy to build the Anti-Gravity Complex.

2003

—The town builds the multi-use Narrow Gauge Pathway.

—The Red Stallion is razed to make way for a housing development.

2008

—Maine Huts & Trails opens its first wilderness hut at Poplar Falls.

2010

—Carrabassett Valley contracts with Hardy Avery of Sustainable Trailworks to develop a plan for a mountain-biking trail system.

—Carrabassett Valley Public Library opens its new building.

2015

—The Samantha Wright Memorial Pool opens at Riverside Park. It is named for the late director of the town's aquatics program.

2016

—The Bill & Joan Alfond Competition Center opens at Sugarloaf.

2020

—Carrabassett Valley's population is 673.

—A large but unknown number of second-home owners retreat to Carrabassett Valley to wait out the COVID-19 pandemic, which shuts down travel, in-office work, and social gatherings around the world.

RESOURCES

Books

Allen, William. *The History of Norridgewock: Comprising Memorials of the Aboriginal Inhabitants and Jesuit Missionaries; Hardships of the Pioneers; Biographical Notices of the Early Settlers; and Ecclesiastical Sketches.* Norridgewock, ME: Edward J. Peet, 1849.

Allis, Frederick S., Jr. *William Bingham's Maine Lands, 1790–1820.* Volumes 36 and 37. Boston: Colonial Society of Massachusetts, 1954.

Banks, Charles Edward. *History of York, Maine, Successively Known as Bristol (1632), Agamentious (1641), Gorgeana (1642), and York (1652).* Baltimore: Regional Pub. Co., 1967.

Barringer, Richard. *A Maine Manifest.* Portland: Tower Publishing Company, 1972.

Calvert, Mary. *Black Robe on the Kennebec.* Monmouth, ME: Monmouth Press, 1991.

Calvert, Mary. *Dawn over the Kennebec.* Lewiston, ME: Twin City Printery, 1983.

Chaplin, Leola Bowie. *The Life and Works of Nathaniel Deering (1791–1881), with the Text of Deering's Plays "Carabasset" and "The Clairvoyants".* Maine Bulletin, August 1934, University of Maine Studies, Second Series, No. 32.

Cook, David. *Above the Gravel Bar: The Native Canoe Routes of Maine.* Milo, ME: Milo Printing Co., 1985.

Cornwall, L. Peter, and Jack W. Farrell. *Ride the Sandy River: Visit the Past on America's Largest Two-Foot Gauge Railroad.* Emerson, WA: Pacific Fast Mail, 1973.

Christie, John. *The Story of Sugarloaf.* Rockport, ME: Down East Books, 2007.

Erickson, Hazel Cushman. *I Grew Up with the Narrow Gauge.* New York: Carlton Press, 1971.

Hanson, John Wesley. *History of the Old Towns, Norridgewock and Canaan: Comprising Norridgewock, Canaan, Starks, Skowhegan, and Bloomfield, from Their Early Settlement to the Year 1849; Including a Sketch of the Abnakis Indians.* Boston: Self-published, 1849.

Huden, John C. *Indian Place Names of New England.* New York: Museum of the American Indian, Here Foundation, 1962.

Hutchins, Curtis Marshall. *Dead River Company: A History, 1907–1972.* Farmington, ME: Knowlton & McLeary, 1972.

Hutchinson, Thomas. *The History of the Province of Massachusetts-Bay, from the Charter of William and Queen Mary, in 1691, until the Year 1750.* London: J. Murray, 1828.

Jones, Robert C. *Two Feet between the Rails, Vol I: The Early Years*. Silverton, CO: Sundance, 1979.

Kidder, Frederic. *The Abenaki Indians, Their Treaties of 1713 & 1717, and a Vocabulary*. Portland, ME: Brown Thurston, 1859.

Krohn, William, and Christopher Hoving. *Early Maine Wildlife*. Orono: University of Maine Press, 2010.

Mastas, Henry L. *Abenaki Indian Legends, Grammar and Place Names*. Victoriaville, Quebec: La Voix des Bois-Francs, 1932.

Moody, Linwood W. *The Maine Two-Footers*. Berkely, CA: Howell-North, 1959.

Orcutt, John and Cynthia. *Enduring Heights: The High Peaks of Maine*. Portland, ME: Carrabassett Publishing, 2017.

Pike, Robert E. *Tall Trees, Tough Men*. New York: W. W. Norton, 1967.

Râle, Father Sebastian. *A Dictionary of the Abnaki Language Published from the Original Manuscript of the Author with an Introductory Memoir and Notes by John Pickering*. Cambridge, MA: C. Folsom, 1833.

Reilly, Wayne E. *Remembering Bangor: The Queen City before the Great Fire*. Charleston, SC: History Press, 2009.

Rioux, Guy. *The Franklin County Narrow Gauges: The Next Stop Is Kingfield*. Boston: Dan Rand Publishing, 2016.

Rioux, Guy. *The Franklin County Narrow Gauges: The Next Stop Is Phillips*. Boston: Dan Rand Publishing, 2014.

Robertston, William. *A General History of America*. London: Mahew, Isaac, & Co., 1834.

Rolde, Neil. *The Uninterrupted Forest: A History of Maine's Wildlands*. Gardiner, ME: Tilbury House, 2001.

Schuyler, Henry C. *A Typical Missionary: Rev. Sebastian Rale, the Apostle of the Abnakis. 1694–1724; Records of the American Catholic Historical Society of Philadelphia* 18, no. 3 (September 1907). American Catholic Historical Society.

Smith, David C. *A History of Lumbering in Maine*. Orono: University of Maine Press, 1972.

Starbird, Charles. *Canibas Indians of the Kennebec*. March 1967.

Walker, Ernest George. *Embden, Town of Yore: Olden Times and Families There and in Adjacent Towns*. Skowhegan, ME: Independent Reporter, 1929.

Workers of the Federal Writers Project of the Works Progress Administration for the State of Maine. *Maine: A Guide Down East*. Boston: Houghton Mifflin, 1937.

Dissertations, Theses, Academic Papers, Scholarly Articles, Letters

Allen, Jill. Interview with Ken Packard. (Walter Trundy, Walter Wallace, Alva Clement, and Lorna [Douglas] Clement, interviewed by Kenneth Whitney, Florence Ireland, Bob Ireland, and Jill Allen. Northeast Archives of Folklore and Oral History,

na0705, courtesy of Fogler Library, University of Maine, https://archives.library
.umaine.edu/repositories/5/archival_objects/355005)

Allen, William. "Bingham Land," *Collections, Maine Historical Society*, Vol. VII (Maine
Historical Society, 1876).

Banfield, Alfred T. "The Padrone, the Sojourners, and the Settlers: A Preface to the
'Little Italies' of Maine." *Maine History* 31, no. 3 (Winter–Spring 1992).

Barringer, Richard, Lee Schepps, Thomas Urquhart, and Martin Wilk. "Maine's Public
Reserved Lands: A Tale of Loss and Recovery." *Maine Policy Review* 29.2 (2020):
65–79. digitalcommons.library.umaine.edu/mpr/vol29/iss2/9.

Begin, Elise. "The Kennebec River: A Historic Maine Resources." Colby College, 2012.

Borns, Harold W., Jr., Lisa A. Doner, Christopher C. Dorion, George L. Jacobson Jr.,
Michael R. Kaplan, Karl J. Kreutz, Thomas V. Lowell, Woodrow B. Thompson, and
Thomas K. Weddle. "The Deglaciation of Maine, USA." Earth Science Faculty,
University of Maine, 2004.

Crittenden, H. T. "Sandy River & Rangely Lakes R.R. System." *Railway and Locomotive
Historical Society Bulletin*, no. 37 (May 1935).

Crommett, Dick. Unpublished articles on Carrabassett history.

Davis, Thelma L. "History of Kingfield" (1933–1934).

Eckstorm, Fannie Hardy. "The Attack on Norridgewock—1724." *New England Quar-
terly* 7, no. 3 (September 1934).

Eckstorm, Fannie Hardy. "Local Indian Place Names 1921" (2018). Fannie Hardy
Eckstorm Papers. Submission 37. digitalcommons.library.umaine.edu/
eckstorm_papers/37.

Osher Map Library. "Antebellum County Maps in Maine: A Social Network." osher-
maps.org.

Siebert, Frank. "Correspondence from Frank Siebert, 1938–1944" (1938). Fannie
Hardy Eckstorm Papers. Submission 12. digitalcommons.library.umaine.edu/
eckstorm_papers/12.

Smith, Ashley Elizabeth. "Remembering Norridgewock: Stories and Politics of a Place
Multiple." Cornell University, 2017.

Waugaman, Elisabeth Pearson. "Names and Identity: The Native American Naming
Tradition." *Psychology Today*, July 8, 2011.

Government Publications, Papers, Studies, and Websites

Carrabassett Valley Connections. Town of Carrabassett Valley.

Carrabassett Valley, Town of. Miscellaneous town meeting and select board minutes.

Clapp, Frederick G. *Underground Waters of Southern Maine with Records of Deep Wells by
W. S. Bayley.* United States Geological Survey, Washington, 1909.

Fontaine, Richard A., and Joseph P. Nielsen. "Flood of April 1987 in Maine." United States Geological Survey Water-Supply Paper 2424, 1994.

Greenleaf, Moses. "A Survey of the State of Maine in Reference to Its Geographical Features, Statistics, and Political Economy 1829" (1829, Moses Greenleaf Papers). digitalmaine.com/moses_greenleaf_papers/9.

Legislature of the State of Maine, 1862. "Address of Governor Washburn to the Legislature of the State of Maine, January 2, 1862."

Maine Geological Survey. "Surficial Geologic History of Maine." October 2005.

Maine Historical Society. "To 1500: People of the Dawn." mainememory.net.

Maine Register, State Year-Book and Legislative Manual, 1873–1874, 1877–1878, 1892–1893, 1893–1894, 1934–1935, 1940–1941, 1942–1943, 1961–1962, 1965–1966.

Maine State Legislature, Law and Legislative Library. legislature.maine.gov/lawlib.

Maine Spruce Budworm Taskforce. "Historical Perspective/Past Infestations." sprucebudwormmaine.org.

Spiess, Arthur. "Maine Native American Pre-European History (or 'Maine Prehistory')." Maine Historic Preservation Commission, January 2018.

Tolman, Andrew L. "Maine Springs." Maine Geological Survey, June 1999.

United States Board on Geographic Names. *Correct Orthography of Geographic Names.* 1911.

United States Bureau of Labor Statistics. "Descriptions of Occupations: Logging Camps and Sawmills, 1918."

U.S. Census Bureau. 2020 American Community Survey.

U.S. Census Bureau. 2020 Decennial Census.

Interviews

Beaupre, John	Folsom-Bell, Elizabeth	Pfeifle, Luke
Begin, Clem	Gilmore, Bill	Rogers, Ed
Begin, Rolande	Harrison, Susan	Rogers, Frank
Cook, Warren	Hoeffler, Liz	Rogers, Meg
Cota, Dave	Howard, Ross	Slagle, John
Cuttler, Lloyd	Jones, Ted	Slagle, Pink
Demshar, Dutch	Knapp, Courtney	Speiss, Arthur
Demshar, Joyce	Karahalios, Nicholas	Tague, Cindy
DiBiase, Andrea	Luce, Jean	Trevor, Ross
DiBiase, John	Luce, Robert	Warren, Larry
Dickey, Herbert	Punderson, Kate Webber	Webber, Peter
Folger, Philip "Brud" Jr.	Punderson, Sam	Wing, Kenny
Fowler, Don	Pfeifle, Hank	

Maps

Baker and Co., J. Chace Jr. & Co., and J. Southwick. *Map of Kennebec Co. 1855.* Philadelphia, 1856.

Chace, J., Jr., and Henry Francis Walling. *Map of Somerset County, 1860.* Portland, ME: J. Chace Jr. & Co., 1861.

Chace, J., Jr., and Henry Francis Walling. *Map of the State of Maine.* Portland, ME: J. Chace Jr. & Co., 1861.

Chace, J., Jr., and Henry Francis Walling. *Map of the State of Maine.* Portland, ME: J. Chace Jr. & Co., 1862.

Colby & Stuart, Wm Bracher, F. Bourquin, and George N. Colby & Co. *Colby's Atlas of Maine, 1886–7.* Houlton, ME: Colby & Stuart, 1887.

J. H. Colton & Co. and C. C Hall. *Colton's Railroad & Township Map of the State of Maine, with Portions of New Hampshire, New Brunswick & Canada.* New York, 1855.

Maine Land Office Plan Book Maps. Plan Book 1, "Survey of Three Townships Adjoining on the West Side of Kennebec River and on the North Line of the Plymouth Company Land." October 1790.

Maine Land Office Plan Book Maps. Plan Book 22, "Survey of the Town of Canaan on a Scale of 200 Rods to an Inch. Includes Boundaries with Norridgewock, Fairfield, and Clinton." June 26, 1794.

Walling, Henry Francis. *Topographical Map of Franklin County, Maine.* New York: W. E. Baker & Co., 1861.

Newspapers, Magazines, and Periodicals

Albion/British Colonial and Foreign Weekly Gazette (New York)
American Advocate (Hallowell)
Bangor Daily News
Bangor Daily Whig & Courier
Bangor Weekly Register
Boston Courier
Boston Daily Advertiser
Boston Globe
Camden Herald
Daily Bulldog
Daily Kennebec Journal (Augusta)
Daily Richmond Whig (Virginia)
Down East
Eastern Times (Bath)
Forest and Stream

Fortune
Independent Reporter (Skowhegan)
Irregular, Original Irregular, and *Sugarloaf Irregular* (Kingfield)
Lewiston Evening Journal
Madison Bulletin
Maine Home and Design
Maine Magazine
Maine Woods (Phillips)
Maine Woodsman (Phillips)
Morning Sentinel (Waterville)
Mountain Ear (North Conway, NH)
Mountain Sports and Living
New England Farmer (Boston)
New York Herald
New York Times

New York Tribune
Oxford Democrat (Paris, ME)
Phillips Phonograph
Portland Advertiser
Portland Daily Press
Rockland Gazette

SKI
Somerset Reporter (Skowhegan)
Sunday Dispatch (New York)
Union and Journal (Biddeford)
Washington Post
Weekly Eastern Argus (Portland)

Websites

A History of Carrabassett Valley, history.carrabassettvalley.org
Carrabassett Region NEMBA, carrabassettnemba.org
Carrabassett Valley Trails, cvtrails.me
Freehub, freehubmag.com
International Skiing History Association, skiinghistory.org
Kingdom Trails, kingdomtrails.com
Maine Emergency Management Agency, State of Maine. maine.gov/mema
Maine Huts & Trails, mainehuts.org
Maine Memory Network, Tell My Story: "Carrabassett Village and the Red Stallion" by David C. Rollins, mainememory.net
Maine Revenue Services, Department of Administrative and Financial Services, maine.gov/revenue
Maine Ski and Snowboard Museum, maineskiandsnowboardmuseum.org
National Weather Service, weather.gov
National Ultra Endurance, Race Series nuemtb.com
Singletracks, singletracks.com
Ski Racing, skiracing.com
Sugarloaf, sugarloaf.com
Sugarloaf Ski Club, sugarloafskiclub.org
U.S. Bureau of Labor Statistics, bls.gov

INDEX

Mills, Janet, 6
Mogul Delicatessen, 104
Moody, Ron, 132–133
Moore, Bob, 162
Morin, Ron, 157, 200, 230
Morris, William W., 33
Morrison, Fred "Buster," 89
Morrison, Lin, 188n49
Morrow, Catherine, 164
Morrow, Steven, 165
Morse, Earle and Pam, 221*f*, 222–223
motto, 3*f*, 109
Mouligne, Patrick, 122
mountain biking, 198*f*–199*f*, 200, 201*f*,
    202–206, 203*f*, 206*f*
Mountain Greenery, 159
Mountainside Real Estate, 169–170
Mount Blue, 92
Mount Katahdin, 61
mud football, 162
Munzer (Bill) Recreational Bridge,
    185*f*, 225
Musello, Frank, 40
music, 100, 130*f*, 132*f*, 133, 136, 138;
    Strunk and, 125–128
Myers, J. H., 77

Nadeau, Roland, 142
Narrow Gauge, 120, 120n39, 123
Narrow Gauge Pathway, 199, 199*f*, 226
National Off-Road Bicycle
    Association, 202
NCAA Ski Championships, 106, 117, 124
New England Governors Ski
    Challenge, 187
New England Mountain Biking
    Association, 200, 202, 204, 225
Nichols, Leslie, 85*f*
Nickerson, Jim, 122, 138
night life, 103, 129–141, 167, 169; Boynton
    and, 170–171; and competitions, 117;

development of, 100; Judson's Inn
    and, 113; law enforcement and, 36;
    and ski jump, 124
Nordic ski touring center, 147*f*, 156–157
Norridgewock, 17–18, 18*f*
North America Pro Ski Tour, 139
Northeast Archaeology Research
    Center, 14
NorthStar EMS, 231
Norton, Leslie, 221

O'Donnell, Joe, 186n48
Orcutt, John and Cynthia, 175
Otten, Les, 184
Outdoor Center, 150*f*, 157, 200, 226, 227
outdoor recreation economy, 3, 9, 90,
    152, 155

Packard, Harvey, 94
Packard, Ken, 25–27, 45, 62, 86, 163
padrone system, 40–41
Page, Robert A., 155
Paleo-Indians, 12–14, 15–16
Parker, Ann van C., 81
Parker, John van, 81–83
partnerships, public/private, 9; Anti-
    Gravity Complex, 197–199,
    197*f*; Carrabassett Valley Trails,
    2*f*, 202–206; and competitions,
    115–123; golf course, 152*f*,
    158–162; Narrow Gauge Pathway,
    199, 199*f*; Nordic ski touring center,
    147*f*, 156–157
partying. *See* night life
Payne, George, 51, 72–74
Peabody, Roger, 115
Peat, Marwick, Mitchell & Co., 176
Pennell, E. L., 57
Penobscot Nation, 6, 19n5, 21, 167,
    173, 236
Pepin, Joe, 114